Academic Encounters

2nd Edition

Jessica Williams
Kristine Brown
Susan Hood
Series Editor: Bernard Seal

CAMBRIDGE
UNIVERSITY PRESS

CAMBRIDGE
UNIVERSITY PRESS

University Printing House, Cambridge CB2 8BS, United Kingdom

One Liberty Plaza, 20th Floor, New York, NY 10006, USA

477 Williamstown Road, Port Melbourne, VIC 3207, Australia

314–321, 3rd Floor, Plot 3, Splendor Forum, Jasola District Centre, New Delhi – 110025, India

79 Anson Road, #06–04/06, Singapore 079906

Cambridge University Press is part of the University of Cambridge.

It furthers the University's mission by disseminating knowledge in the pursuit of education, learning and research at the highest international levels of excellence.

www.cambridge.org
Information on this title: www.cambridge.org/9781107658325

© Cambridge University Press 2012

First published 2004
Second edition 2012

40 39 38 37 36 35 34 33 32 31 30 29 28 27 26 25 24 23 22 21

Printed in Mexico by Editorial Impresora Apolo, S.A. de C.V.

A catalogue record for this publication is available from the British Library

Library of Congress Cataloging in Publication Data

Williams, Jessica, 1957-
[Academic listening encounters]
Academic encounters, life in society, level 3 : reading and writing / Jessica Williams, Kristine Brown, Susan Hood. -- 2nd ed.
p. cm. -- (Academic encounters. Life in society)
Previous ed.: 2002.
Includes index.
ISBN 978-1-107-65832-5 (Student's book)
1. English language--Textbooks for foreign speakers. 2. English language--Rhetoric. 3. Social problems-- Problems, exercises, etc. 4. Readers--Social problems. 5. Academic writing. I. Brown, Kristine. II. Hood, Susan. III. Title.

PE1128.W7255 2012
428.2'4--dc23

2012012505

ISBN 978-1-107-65832-5 Student's Book
ISBN 978-1-107-63137-3 Teacher's Manual

Additional resources for this publication at www.cambridge.org/academicencounters

Art direction, book design, and photo research: Integra
Layout services: Integra

Table of Contents

Scope and sequence

Unit 1: Belonging to a Group • 1

	Content	R Reading Skills	W Writing Skills
Chapter 1 **Marriage, Family, and the Home** page 4	**Reading 1** Marriage: A Changing Institution **Reading 2** The Family Today **Reading 3** How We Learn to Behave	Examining graphics Reading for main ideas Reading actively Skimming Thinking about the topic Predicting Personalizing the topic Reading boxed texts Applying what you have read	Writing about changes Definitions
Chapter 2 **The Power of the Group** page 28	**Reading 1** The Influence of Culture **Reading 2** Peer Groups **Reading 3** Crowds	Thinking about the topic Reading actively Understanding key terms Personalizing the topic Previewing art Skimming Applying what you have read	Expanded definitions Describing differences Understanding text structure

Unit 2: Gender in Society • 53

	Content	R Reading Skills	W Writing Skills
Chapter 3 **Gender Roles** page 56	**Reading 1** Growing up Male or Female **Reading 2** Gender and Academic Achievement **Reading 3** The Influence of Mass Media on Gender Roles	Skimming Personalizing the topic Examining graphics Predicting Reading for main ideas Applying what you have read Thinking about the topic Increasing reading speed Reading for details	Showing contrast Summarizing Using adverbs The passive voice
Chapter 4 **Gender Issues Today** page 82	**Reading 1** Balancing Home and Work **Reading 2** It's Not So Easy Being Male **Reading 3** Gender Equality at Work	Thinking about the topic Reading for details Personalizing the topic Skimming Previewing art Predicting Reading for main ideas Thinking critically	Pronoun reference Going beyond the text Supporting main ideas

V Vocabulary Skills	A Academic Success Skills	Learning Outcomes
Words related to the topic Guessing meaning from context Word families	Taking notes Answering short-answer questions	
Collocations Synonyms Using grammar to guess meaning Describing behavior	Organizational phrases Organizing your notes in outline form Copying a lecturer's diagrams and charts	Write a two-paragraph essay illustrating the power of the group

V Vocabulary Skills	A Academic Success Skills	Learning Outcomes
Cues for finding word meaning Describing people	Making a chart Answering short-answer test questions	
Word families Describing personality and emotion Guessing meaning from context Collocations	Responding to a quote Answering definition questions on a test	Write a "Yes, but . . . " essay about whether it is better to be a man or a woman

Unit 3: Media and Society • 109

	Content	Ⓡ Reading Skills	Ⓦ Writing Skills
Chapter 5 **Mass Media Today** page 112	**Reading 1** The Role of Mass Media **Reading 2** What Is Newsworthy? **Reading 3** Privacy and the Media	Personalizing the topic Reading for details Skimming Thinking about the topic Applying what you have read Reading boxed texts Predicting	Linking ideas in a text Summarizing Road map sentences
Chapter 6 **Impact of the Media on Our Lives** page 134	**Reading 1** The Impact of the Internet on Mass Media **Reading 2** Social Media **Reading 3** Learning and Thinking with New Media	Scanning Increasing reading speed Reading for main ideas Skimming Previewing art and graphics Personalizing the topic	Going beyond the text

Unit 4: Breaking the Rules • 161

	Content	Ⓡ Reading Skills	Ⓦ Writing Skills
Chapter 7 **Crime and Criminals** page 164	**Reading 1** Deviance and Crime **Reading 2** Who Commits Crime? **Reading 3** Technology and Crime	Thinking about the topic Scanning Understanding cartoons Reading critically Reading for main ideas	The passive voice Comparing data Going beyond the text
Chapter 8 **Controlling Crime** page 188	**Reading 1** What Stops Us from Committing Crimes? **Reading 2** Science and Technology in Crime Fighting **Reading 3** Crime and Punishments	Personalizing the topic Increasing reading speed Applying what you have read Thinking about the topic Reading for details	Using data from a graphic Signals of chronological order

V Vocabulary Skills	**A Academic Success Skills**	**Learning Outcomes**
Words related to the topic The Academic Word List Compound words and phrases Collocations	Highlighting Answering true/false questions	Write an essay on media use based on a survey
Prefixes and suffixes The Academic Word List Collocations Guessing meaning from context	Answering multiple-choice questions Preparing for an essay test	

V Vocabulary Skills	**A Academic Success Skills**	**Learning Outcomes**
Words related to the topic Guessing meaning from context Synonyms Collocations	Answering short-answer test questions	Write an essay based on a prompt
Verbs of control Word families The Academic Word List Collocations	Highlighting Making a chart	

Academic Encounters: Preparing Students for Academic Coursework

The Series

Academic Encounters is a sustained content-based series for English language learners preparing to study college-level subject matter in English. The goal of the series is to expose students to the types of texts and tasks that they will encounter in their academic coursework and provide them with the skills to be successful when that encounter occurs.

Academic Content

At each level in the series, there are two thematically paired books. One is an academic reading and writing skills book, in which students encounter readings that are based on authentic academic texts. In this book, students are given the skills to understand texts and respond to them in writing. The reading and writing book is paired with an academic listening and speaking skills book, in which students encounter interview and lecture material specially prepared by experts in their field. In this book, students learn how to take notes from a lecture, participate in discussions, and prepare short oral presentations.

Flexibility

The books at each level may be used as stand-alone reading and writing books or listening and speaking books. They may also be used together to create a complete four-skills course. This is made possible because the content of each book at each level is very closely related. Each unit and chapter, for example, has the same title and deals with similar content, so that teachers can easily focus on different skills, but the similar content, as they toggle from one book to the other. Additionally, if the books are taught together, when students are presented with the culminating unit writing or speaking assignment, they will have a rich and varied supply of reading and lecture material to draw on.

A Sustained Content Approach

A sustained content approach teaches language through the study of subject matter from one or two related academic content areas. This approach simulates the experience of university courses and better prepares students for academic study.

Students benefit from a sustained content approach

Real-world academic language and skills
Students learn how to understand and use academic language because they are studying actual academic content.

An authentic, intensive experience
By immersing students in the language of a single academic discipline, sustained content helps prepare them for the rigor of later coursework.

Natural recycling of language
Because a sustained content course focuses on a particular academic discipline, concepts and language naturally recur. As students progress through the course, their ability to work with authentic language improves dramatically.

Knowledge of common academic content
When students work with content from the most popular university courses, they gain real knowledge of these academic disciplines. This helps them to be more successful when they move on to later coursework.

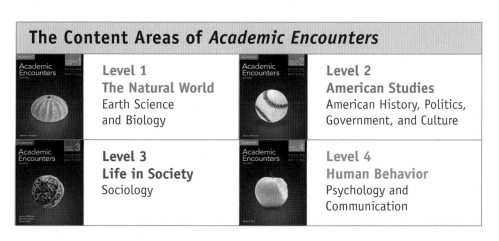

The Content Areas of *Academic Encounters*

Level 1 **The Natural World** Earth Science and Biology	**Level 2** **American Studies** American History, Politics, Government, and Culture
Level 3 **Life in Society** Sociology	**Level 4** **Human Behavior** Psychology and Communication

Academic Skills

Academic Encounters teaches skills in four main areas. A set of icons highlights which skills are practiced in each exercise.

R Reading Skills

The reading skills tasks are designed to help students develop strategies before reading, while reading, and after reading.

W Writing Skills

Students learn how to notice and analyze written texts, develop critical writing skills, and apply these in longer writing tasks. These skills and tasks were carefully selected to prepare students for university study.

V Vocabulary Development

Vocabulary learning is an essential part of improving one's ability to read an academic text. Tasks throughout the books focus on particular sets of vocabulary that are important for reading in a specific subject area as well as vocabulary from the Academic Word List.

A Academic Success

Besides learning how to read, write, and build their language proficiency, students also have to learn other skills that are particularly important in academic settings. These include skills such as learning how to prepare for a content test, answering certain types of test questions, taking notes, and working in study groups.

Learning to read academic content

PREPARING TO READ

1 Thinking about the topic ℝ

A Think about how men and women are portrayed in different types of mass media. Make some notes in the chart below.

Type of Media	Women	Men
Television		
Movies		
Magazines		
Computer games		

B Discuss what you have written in the chart with your classmates.

2 Increasing reading speed ℝ

College students often have very long reading assignments. They need to develop a fast reading style. A good goal is to read about 250 words per minute. To increase your reading speed, use the following techniques.
- Try to focus on groups of words, not on individual words.
- Try not to backtrack (go over the text again and again).
- Guess at the general meaning of words that you do not know.
- Skip over words that you do not know and that do not seem very important.
- Slow down slightly for key information, such as definitions and main ideas.
- Speed up for less important information, such as examples and details.

A Quickly read the text on the next page using these techniques.

B Calculate your reading speed.

Write your reading time _____
Number of words: 1,012 words
Divide the number of words by your time.
Write your speed: _____ words/minute

Differences across cultures

40 It is easy to assume that every culture socializes children in the same way. Research studies, however, show that there are cross-cultural differences in what families expect of their children and in how they socialize them to behave appropriately. For example, in some Asian families the needs of the group are traditionally 45 seen as more important than the needs of the individual. Children learn that their first responsibility is to their parents rather than to themselves. For example, many children work hard at school so that their parents will be proud of them.

There are also differences in the amount of responsibility 50 children are expected to take within their families, and this has an important effect on their behavior. A study of six- to eleven-year-old children in six communities in the United States, Kenya, Japan, India, the Philippines, and Mexico revealed a considerable difference across these cultures in the level of responsibility children had. The children 55 in Kenya and Mexico were expected to take care of the other younger children in the family and do household chores that helped the whole family. These children quickly learned to be responsible and caring toward others. Parental expectations about work around the house were an important part of children's socialization. In contrast, in the 60 United States, children had fewer chores, and they were less likely to develop these traits at an early age. All of these forms of socialization determine how we behave when we become adults.

"Tiger Mother"

Socialization of children often remains an important part of a culture even when the group's circumstances change. For example, in many Asian-American homes, the importance of hard work, achievement, and respect for family still plays a key role in socialization of children. In 2010, Amy Chua, a Chinese-American, shocked many American readers when she described

Amy Chua

the way she raised her two daughters. She calls herself a "Tiger Mother." She was very strict with them. She didn't let them watch television or go to their friends' houses to play. She forced one of her daughters to do 2,000 math problems every night until she was the best in the class. She said she would burn her daughter's dolls if she did not play her music perfectly. Her daughters are top students and have won many musical competitions.

The Structure of Academic Text

B With a partner, discuss the terms in the sentences below. If you do not know these words, look them up in a dictionary. Pay special attention to the prepositions that occur with the verbs. Put these seven actions in the order in which you would expect them to occur. Put the correct number from 1 through 7 in the blank.

___ The offender is **convicted of** the crime.

___ The person is **arrested for** the crime.

___ The crime is **investigated by** the police.

___ A person **commits** a crime.

___ The offender is **sentenced to** time in prison.

___ The person is **charged with** the crime.

___ The person is **tried for** the crime.

C Read the true story of the serial killer, Thierry Paulin. Use the words in the box to fill in the blanks. In some cases, use your knowledge of collocations from Step B to help you choose. You will need to use some of the words more than once.

tried	investigated	arrested
charged	sentenced	convicted

Thierry Paulin was a serial killer in France in the 1980s. His first crime was in 1982. He robbed an elderly woman in a grocery store. He was _____ for the crime a few days later, and he was _____ with robbery. He was _____ of the crime and _____ to two years in prison. However, the sentence was suspended, which means he never had to spend any time in prison. He continued his life of crime, but his crimes became more serious. Between 1984 and 1987, he killed at least 18 elderly people and assaulted many others. The police _____ these crimes, but Paulin did not leave much evidence when he attacked his victims. Finally, one of his victims survived, and she was able to describe Paulin to the police. Soon after, the police _____ him and _____ him with several of the murders. However, he became very sick and died in prison in 1988 before he was _____ for these terrible crimes.

> **Extensive scaffolding** activities teach students the **structure of academic writing**.

> Students learn **key writing skills** such as summarizing and avoiding plagiarism. This early focus **prepares students** for later extended writing tasks.

Reading 2

SCIENCE AND TECHNOLOGY IN CRIME FIGHTING

law enforcement agencies
government offices that are responsible for upholding laws and finding people who break them

Even effective controls cannot prevent all crimes. Therefore, when crimes do occur, society must have a way to find out who has committed them. The first step in enforcing the law is detection, in other words, solving the crime. **Law enforcement agencies** have been
5 working to solve crimes for many years. It is a challenging job, but in recent history, *forensics* – the use of science and technology to solve crimes – has become an important tool.

Fingerprints

Probably the most important advance in forensics in the past century is the widespread use of fingerprints for identification. A person's
10 fingerprints are the swirled patterns on the skin at the tips of the fingers. These patterns do not change over time, and they can be used to identify people. Fingerprints are made when someone touches a surface. Sweat and acids from the body transfer to the surface and leave a mark. Sometimes it is only a partial fingerprint, but that can
15 be sufficient to make an identification. Many fingerprints are invisible under normal circumstances, but they can be made visible with special chemicals. Prints can also be examined in darkness using high-powered lasers, and they can be retrieved from almost any surface – even clothing, plastic bags, or human skin.

20   Law enforcement agencies all over the world have large collections of fingerprints to aid in crime detection. These have been computerized to make it easier to search for matching prints. If fingerprints are found at a crime scene, they can be compared with the fingerprints stored in a computer bank. However, fingerprint matching is not as
25 reliable as many people believe. For a long time, it was believed that everyone had a unique set of fingerprints. Experts are still debating this claim, but one thing is clear: both people and machines can make mistakes. In 2004, a lawyer in Oregon was arrested for participation in the bombing of a train in Madrid based on a fingerprint. It was later
30 discovered the match was a mistake. Mistakes like this can ruin the lives of innocent people.

Immersive Skill Building

Additional Suffixes and Their Meanings			
Prefix	Meaning	Example	Part of speech
-er/or	*Xer* is someone or something that/who does X	writer	noun
-ive	Something that is *Xive* is concerned with/characterized by X	active	adjective
-cy	*Xcy* is the state of being X	democracy	noun
-ous	*Xous* means full of X	dangerous	adjective
-ful	*Xful* means full of X	forceful	adjective

A Look at the words in the chart below. Fill the blanks with words from the reading that contain suffixes.

Noun	Verb	Adjective
expense		_____
_____	browse	
familiarity		_____
availability		_____
_____	interact	
_____		accurate
	rely	_____
caution		_____
power		_____
_____	consume	
mass		_____
_____		minor

Chapter 6 *Impact of the Media*

The full-color **design mirrors university textbooks**, ensuring that students not only practice reading authentic texts, but also receive an **authentic university experience**.

B Read the sentences with the boldface words. Then discuss with your classmates which is a more likely conclusion, *a* or *b*.

1. His mother **suspected** he had been smoking.
   a. She smelled smoke on his clothes.   b. She saw him with a cigarette.
2. He decided to **withdraw** $600 to pay for his computer.
   a. He went to the computer store.   b. He went to the bank.
3. The students gathered economic **data** about different countries for their project.
   a. They went to the library.   b. They asked their parents.
4. In the United States, government **agencies** are closed on Sundays.
   a. The Post Office and passport office are closed on Sundays.
   b. The White House is closed on Sundays.
5. She **deposited** her paycheck yesterday.
   a. The amount in her bank account is larger today.
   b. The amount in her bank account is smaller today.
6. The police found a large supply of **counterfeit** watches.
   a. The police are going to buy the watches.
   b. The police are going to destroy the watches.
7. The computer in the company's main office **transmits** information about products to their other offices.
   a. Managers in all of the offices have up-to-date information.
   b. The managers in all of the offices only want the most important information.
8. She **made** so many **purchases** that she had to take a taxi home.
   a. Her bags were heavy.   b. The taxi was expensive.
9. We have to move the equipment inside **rapidly**. A storm is coming.
   a. The storm will bring heavy rain and wind tomorrow.
   b. The storm is very close.
10. She keeps all of her important papers in a **secure** location.
    a. Her papers are in a locked box.   b. Her papers are in another country.

3 Collocations Ⓥ Ⓡ

You have learned that some verbs typically collocate with specific nouns and others collocate with specific prepositions. In addition, some collocate with a noun *and* a preposition in the same phrase.

Throughout each unit, **explanatory boxes describe each skill** and help **students understand why it is important.**

Academic Vocabulary and Writing

Chapter 1 Academic Vocabulary Review

The following words appear in the readings in Chapter 1. They all come from the Academic Word List, a list of words that researchers have discovered occur frequently in many different types of academic texts. For a complete list of all the Academic Word List words in this chapter and in all the readings in this book, see the Appendix on pages 213–214.

Reading 1 Marriage: A Changing Institution	Reading 2 The Family Today	Reading 3 How We Learn to Behave
adapt	affect	appropriately
community	conflict (n)	assume
eventually	consist	circumstances
experts	couples	negative
immigrate	image	positive
variation	incomes	task

Complete the sentences with words from the lists.

1. Some _____ wait until they have saved enough money before they marry.
2. People with higher _____ can buy more things, but they are not always happier than people with less money.
3. People who are following norms behave _____ in most situations.
4. _____ give several different reasons for why the age of first marriage has risen in the last 50 years.
5. It is important not to _____ that you know other people's opinions before you ask them.
6. In the past, many people had a _____ opinion about women who did not marry. Today, this has changed, and more women are choosing to remain single.
7. People often choose to _____ to another country for economic and political reasons.
8. Blended families can create _____ among family members until everyone adjusts to the new arrangement.
9. Learning to write in a new language is a difficult _____ .
10. New immigrants must learn to _____ to the customs of their new countries.
11. If you work hard and are patient, _____ you will reach your goals.
12. There is _____ in family structure across different countries and cultures. Families are not the same everywhere.

Chapter 1 *Marriage, Family, and the Ho...*

Academic vocabulary development is **critical to student success**. Each unit includes **intensive vocabulary practice**, including words from the Academic Word List.

Students complete each unit by **applying their skills** and knowledge in an extended writing task that **replicates university coursework.**

AFTER YOU WRITE

A Reread your draft and check that:
- It has an introductory paragraph with a general statement and a main idea sentence that states a claim about the topic.
- Each body paragraph has a topic sentence and supporting evidence.
- It has an appropriate conclusion.

Transitions

Writing good paragraphs is important, but it is also important to make sure the paragraphs all fit well together. One way to help all of the pieces fit well is to write a sentence that makes a good transition between one paragraph and another. Good writers try to create a thread that connects the end of one paragraph to the beginning of the next. They may repeat a word or use a synonym to show the connection between the two paragraphs.
Kinds of Connections
- Sometimes each paragraph is an item on a **list**, for example, each paragraph gives a reason or an example. The first sentence in each paragraph may include words such as *first, second,* or *most important.*
- Sometimes there is a **contrast** between the two paragraphs. The first sentence in the second paragraph may show this contrast with something in the previous paragraph.
- Sometimes the first paragraph contains a statement, and the next paragraph contains an **explanation** or **expansion** of the statement.
- Sometimes one paragraph presents a **problem** and the next paragraph offers a **solution**.
- Sometimes the relationship between the paragraphs is **cause** and **effect**. The first sentence in the second paragraph may show this relationship.

B Read the text below. Pay special attention to the words in red in the first and last sentences. Describe the connection between the two paragraphs. Write it on the blank line to the left of the paragraph. The first one is done for you.

> Forensics is an important part of the criminal justice system. It is the use of science and technology to solve crimes. We think of forensics as a high-tech field with lots of special tools and machines, but actually it has a long history.
>
> *expansion*____ The use of science to solve a crime dates back at least 700 years. A Chinese book showed the physical differences between a victim of drowning and a victim of strangulation. Almost 600 years later, in the early 1800s, a Spanish chemist published a book about poisons and how to identify them inside a person's body. In the 1880s, fingerprints began to be used as evidence in crimes. At that time, the techniques and equipment were not very advanced.

Chapter 8 *Controlling Crime* **211**

To the student

Welcome to *Academic Encounters 3 Reading and Writing: Life in Society*!

The *Academic Encounters* series gets its name because in this series you will encounter, or meet, the kinds of *academic* texts (lectures and readings), *academic* language (grammar and vocabulary), and *academic* tasks (taking tests, writing papers, and giving presentations) that you will encounter when you study an academic subject area in English. The goal of the series, therefore, is to prepare you for that encounter.

The approach of *Academic Encounters 3 Reading and Writing: Life in Society* may be different from what you are used to in your English studies. In this book, you are asked to study an academic subject area and be responsible for learning that information, in the same way as you might study in a college or university course. You will find that as you study this information, you will at the same time improve your English language proficiency and develop the skills that you will need to be successful when you come to study in your own academic subject area in English.

In *Academic Encounters 3 Reading and Writing: Life in Society*, for example, you will learn:

- how to read academic texts
- ways to think critically about what you read
- how to write in an academic style
- methods of preparing for tests
- strategies for dealing with new vocabulary
- note-taking and study techniques

This course is designed to help you study in English in *any* subject matter. However, because during the study of this book, you will learn a lot of new information about research findings and theories in the field of sociology, you may feel that by the end you have enough background information to one day take and be successful in an introductory course in sociology in English.

We certainly hope that you find *Academic Encounters 3 Reading and Writing: Life in Society* useful. We also hope that you will find it to be enjoyable. It is important to remember that the most successful learning takes place when you enjoy what you are studying and find it interesting.

Author's acknowledgments

First and foremost, I would like to thank Kristine Brown and Susan Hood for providing such a rich and interesting text in the first edition. It made revision for the second edition both a pleasure and a learning experience.

Thanks, too, to Bernard Seal, series editor, for bringing me in on the project, and for his advice throughout the revision process. It is a process that has seen the helping hand of many others, who also deserve my gratitude and appreciation. These include Christopher Sol Cruz, Larry Zwier, Brandon Carda, Robin Berenbaum, and the staff at Cambridge University Press.

Jessica Williams

Publisher's acknowledgments

The first edition of *Academic Encounters* has been used by many teachers in many institutions all around the world. Over the years, countless instructors have passed on feedback about the series, all of which has proven invaluable in helping to direct the vision for the second edition. More formally, a number of reviewers also provided us with a detailed analysis of the series, and we are especially grateful for their insights. We would therefore like to extend particular thanks to the following instructors:

Matthew Gordon Ray Courtney, The University of Auckland, New Zealand

Nancy Hamadou, Pima Community College – West Campus, Tucson, AZ

Yoneko Kanaoka, Hawaii English Language Program at the University of Hawaii at Manoa;
    Honolulu, Hawaii

Margaret V. Layton, University of Nevada, Reno, Nevada

Dot MacKenzie, Kuwait University, Sabah Al-Salem University City, Kuwait

Jennifer Wharton, Leeward Community College, Pearl City, Hawaii

Unit 1
Belonging to a Group

In this unit you will look at the different ways in which human beings are part of larger groups. In Chapter 1 you will focus on families – different types of families and households, and their importance in developing our social skills and behaviors. In Chapter 2 you will look beyond the family. First, you will examine the role of culture in general, and then you will look at one very influential group within most cultures: the peer group. You will also look at an example of collective, or group, behavior – the behavior of people when they are part of a crowd.

Contents

In Unit 1, you will read and write about the following topics.

Skills

In Unit 1, you will practice the following skills.

R Reading Skills

Examining graphics
Reading for main ideas
Reading actively
Skimming
Thinking about the topic
Predicting
Personalizing the topic
Reading boxed texts
Applying what you have read
Understanding key terms
Previewing art

W Writing Skills

Writing about changes
Definitions
Expanded definitions
Describing differences
Understanding text structure
Writing a body paragraph

V Vocabulary Skills

Words related to the topic
Guessing meaning from context
Word families
Collocations
Synonyms
Using grammar to guess meaning
Describing behavior

A Academic Success Skills

Taking notes
Answering short-answer questions
Reviewing for a test

Learning Outcomes

Write a two-paragraph essay illustrating the power of the group.

Previewing the Unit

Before reading a unit (or chapter) of a textbook, it is a good idea to preview the contents page and to think about the topics that will be covered. This will give you an overview of how the unit is organized and what it is going to be about.

Read the contents page for Unit 1 on page 2 and do the following activities.

Chapter 1: Marriage, Family, and the Home

A The first two sections of Chapter 1 look at marriage and different types of families and households. Work with a partner and explain what each of the following terms probably means:

- arranged marriage
- single-person households
- divorce rate
- nuclear family
- blended family
- boomerang children

B Section 3 of this chapter focuses on how children learn to take their part in society. Write down five to ten things that are considered to be good behavior for children from your own point of view (e.g., saying "thank you" when they are given something). Then discuss the following question with your classmates:

How do people generally try to teach these behaviors?

Chapter 2: The Power of the Group

A Chapter 2 looks at what influences people's social behavior. Look at these pictures and discuss the following question with your classmates:

How likely are you to see people doing these things in your country or community?

B In this chapter you will learn that people belong to many different social groups besides their families. Make a list of the different social groups to which you belong (e.g., sports team, school, or neighborhood).

Chapter 1
Marriage, Family, and the Home

PREPARING TO READ

1 Words related to the topic ⓥ

The title of the text refers to marriage as an *institution*. This word has many different meanings. For sociologists, it has the following definition:

a custom or tradition that has existed for a long time and is accepted as an important part of a particular society

Discuss the following with a classmate.

1. After you have studied the definition, decide if you think marriage is an *institution*.

2. What are some other examples of cultural or social institutions?

2 Examining graphics ⓡ

Before reading a text, it is helpful to look at any graphs, tables (sometimes called charts), or diagrams. These will give you an idea of the content of the text.

Look at the graphs in this text (Figures 1.1 and 1.2) and read the words that explain them. With a partner, answer the questions below in your own words.

1. What does Figure 1.1 show?

2. What do the points along the *y* axis (the vertical line) in Figure 1.1 represent?

3. What does Figure 1.2 show?

4. What do the points along the *x* axis (the horizontal line) in Figure 1.2 represent?

5. Does the information in Figure 1.1 surprise you? Why or why not?

6. Does the information in Figure 1.2 surprise you? Why or why not?

Reading 1

MARRIAGE: A CHANGING INSTITUTION

In the movies, we often watch two young people who meet and fall in love. After a while, they decide to get married, they start a family, and they live happily ever after. Sometimes it happens this way, but not always. Not all young people fall in love and get married. Not
5 everyone who gets married lives happily ever after. Although some people get married for love, people marry for other reasons as well.

Some people marry for economic or political reasons. In some societies, a marriage is traditionally a union between families rather than individuals. In many countries, particularly in Asia, these
10 *arranged marriages* are still quite common. This means that the parents decide whom their child will marry. They often choose a young man or woman from the same community with a similar background because they believe this kind of marriage will be successful. In most, but not all, cases, the young people also participate in the decision.
15 They are not forced to marry if they do not want to.

Arranged marriages are common in many parts of the world.

Although there is variation across cultures, marriage is an institution in almost every culture, and most people do get married. In most countries, more than 90 percent of people get married at some time during their lives. The age of first marriage has risen in the last

20 century. In the United States, the **median age** at which people marry for the first time has risen from 22.8 for men and 20.3 for women in 1960 to 28.2 for men and 26.1 for women in 2010. This trend is not limited to the United States. The numbers in many countries around the world, especially in western countries, are similar (see Figure 1.1).

Figure 1.1. Marriage trends by country

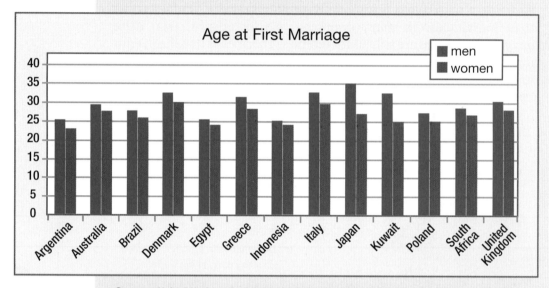

Source: United Nations: Population Division (based on latest figures available in 2010)

Staying single

25 These data indicate that many people in these countries are staying single until they are older. These young adults – the majority of them are women – postpone marriage until their late twenties and thirties or even forties. One reason they often give for staying single is that they have not met the right person. Others say that marriage involves
30 too much responsibility or that they simply like being single. They are free to spend their money and time as they wish. They are free to start new relationships or end old ones. In short, they can make their own decisions.

There are also two important sociological reasons for this
35 increase in the number of young singles. First, the social pressure to get married has declined. Fifty years ago, young women who did not marry might have felt embarrassed and ashamed. Today, they

can have close, meaningful relationships without marriage. More important, the opportunity for single people to have a good life has
40 expanded. This is especially true for women. As educational and employment opportunities for women have increased, marriage is no longer the only path to economic security, emotional support, and social respectability.

It is not only young people who are single, however. It is
45 increasingly common for people of all ages. This includes people who have never married as well as people who are no longer married because they are divorced or their spouses have died. As a result, in the last 20 years, the number of *single-person households* has grown significantly. In Australia, for example, almost one quarter of the
50 population lives alone. The figure in the United States is even higher – almost 30 percent. In many European countries, it is higher still. In Germany and England, this figure is close to 40 percent. This trend is particularly clear in large cities, where almost half of all households have just one person.

The divorce rate

55 There has been a considerable increase in the *divorce rate* all over the world in the last seventy-five years. In the United States, it reached a
60 high point in the 1980s. It has declined somewhat since then, but it remains the highest rate in the world. About 40 percent of all American marriages
65 eventually end in divorce. Divorce has also become relatively common in Russia and the United Kingdom (see Figure 1.2). Even in countries
70 such as India, where the divorce rate has traditionally been low, the rate doubled between 2005 and 2010.

Figure. 1.2. Divorce rates by country

Source: Nationmaster (based on latest available figures for each country in 2010)

What can explain this widespread increase in the divorce rate? Experts give several reasons. First, social disapproval of divorce has decreased. At one time, many people stayed in unhappy marriages
75 because divorce was unacceptable in their communities. Now, divorce is more acceptable. Second, women often stayed married for economic reasons. Divorce could mean a life of poverty for them because they had no way to earn money for themselves. This is no longer true in many countries. This is related to a third reason for the rise in divorce.

80 As the economic reasons for marriage have become less important, the emotional reasons for marriage have become primary. As a result, when two people no longer love each other, there may not be a good reason for them to remain in the marriage. Finally, the laws in many countries have changed to make it easier to get divorced.

Customized Speed-Dating

In many Muslim communities, parents play an important role in choosing whom their children will marry. When Muslims immigrate to countries such as the United States, where they are a minority, this process becomes more challenging. Pakistani-American Jamal Mohsin thinks he has a solution. In 2007 he adapted *speed-dating* to the Muslim context. Normally, speed-dating takes place in bars. Young people talk to their "date" for about 5 minutes and then they move on to the next "date." This continues all evening. They hope to find someone they like. If they like each other in their 5-minute "date," they might agree to meet again.

Muslim speed-dating does not occur in a bar. Instead, it takes place in a hotel conference room, and the parents of the young women are watching and taking notes. The event has become popular with the Muslim community in New York and attracts Muslim-Americans from all over the country. As of 2011, there have been twenty-six weddings among those who have participated.

1 Reading for main ideas ⓡ

> Understanding the main idea of the whole text is an important reading skill in
> college. Two strategies that will help you identify the main idea of a text are:
> • reading the introductory paragraph of the text
> • paying attention to the headings that organize the text

Reread the introductory paragraph (Par. 1) and headings of "Marriage: A Changing
Institution." Read the four sentences that follow. Then choose the sentence that best
states the main idea of the text.

> **a.** Marriage is an almost universal institution.
>
> **b.** The traditional institution of marriage has changed in a variety of ways.
>
> **c.** Young people everywhere are still falling in love and getting married.
>
> **d.** Marriage has many different functions in different cultures.

2 Reading actively ⓡ

> When you read you should be doing more than simply taking in the words on the
> page. To understand a text well and to remember what you have read, you need
> to read actively. One way to read actively is to respond to the cues that the author
> provides to follow the argument in the text, especially when you are studying for a
> test. You many need to read a text more than once. As you read, use the cues to
> ask yourself questions:

Cue	Question
One reason, purpose, function	What is the second, third, etc., reason, function, purpose?
There are other reasons, functions, uses	What are they? Did the author already name one?
In some cases, X happens	What happens in other cases?
As a result	What was the cause? Did I miss that?
Not only	What else? Who else?
There are two/three/several . . . reasons, types	What are they? Did the author number them?
Finally,	What were the first one, two? Did I miss them?

A Find examples of these cues in "Marriage: A Changing Institution." Underline them.

B Ask yourself the questions that go with each cue. Find the answer in the text and highlight it. An example is provided below.

It is <u>not only</u> young people who are single, however. It is increasingly common for <mark>people of all ages.</mark>

3 Guessing meaning from context Ⓥ Ⓡ

It is important to develop strategies for dealing with difficult or unfamiliar vocabulary in the texts you read. One important strategy is looking at the context (that is, the words and sentences that come before and after the unknown word) for clues to the word's meaning.

Read the sentences from the text. Try to figure out the meaning of the word in bold from the context. The words in italics may help you figure out its meaning. Circle the word or words that have a similar meaning.

1. In some societies, a marriage is traditionally a union between *families rather than* **individuals**.
   a. members   b. complete strangers   c. single people

2. This includes people who have never married as well as people who are *no longer married* either because they are divorced or their **spouses** have died.
   a. mother or father   b. son or daughter   c. husband or wife

3. The *age of first marriage has risen* in the last century. In the United States, the median age at which people marry for the first time has risen from 22.8 for men and 20.3 for women in 1960 to 28.2 for men and 26.1 for women in 2010. This **trend** is not limited to the United States.
   a. development   b. number   c. age

4. These young adults – the majority of them are women – **postpone** marriage *until* their late twenties and thirties and even forties.
   a. attempt   b. expect   c. delay

5. Second, women often stayed married for economic reasons. Divorce could mean a life of **poverty** for them because they had *no way to earn money for themselves*.
   a. working hard   b. being poor   c. being ashamed

6. As the economic reasons for marriage have become *less important*, the emotional reasons for marriage have become **primary**.
   a. more restrictive   b. more likely   c. most important

4 Writing about changes Ⓦ Ⓡ

College textbooks often include texts (like "Marriage: A Changing Institution") about changes over a period of time. Some common ways to describe changes over time are shown in the tables:

	Adverb	Adjective
has become / became	less somewhat relatively fairly increasingly more quite	common frequent rare unusual

	Adjective	Noun
there has been a / there was a	slight considerable significant	increase decrease rise fall

Verb	Adverb or Adverb Phrase
(has) increased (has) decreased has gone up (or down) / went up (or down) has risen has grown has fallen	considerably significantly somewhat a little (by) X percent

	Quantity Verb
(has) almost (has) more than	doubled tripled

A Find examples of some of these language patterns in the text.

B Use some of the language patterns to write two sentences about the graph (Figure 1.3).

Fig. 1.3. Marriage and divorce rates by country: 1980 to 2005

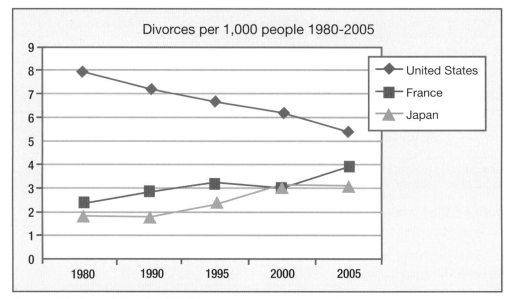

Source: U.S. Census International Statistics

1. _____

_____

2. _____

_____

1 Skimming ®

Skimming a text before you read it will make the text easier to understand. Skimming means looking quickly over a text to get an idea of what it is about and of how it is organized. You should not read every word. Instead, you should look at headings, pictures, graphs, and highlighted words. It is also a good idea to read the introduction and the first sentence of each paragraph.

A Give yourself one minute to skim the text "The Family Today." Without looking back, write down the headings you saw.

B Give yourself another minute to skim the text. Without looking back, write down some key words you remember.

C Reread the introduction to the text (Par. 1) and then check (✓) the phrase that best describes what you think this text will be about.

_____ **a.** Similarities and differences in families in the United States and other countries

_____ **b.** New kinds of family arrangements

_____ **c.** The changing roles of mothers in the family

_____ **d.** The disappearance of traditions and cultural customs

2 Thinking about the topic ®

The text "The Family Today" examines new kinds of family units. Discuss the questions with your classmates:

1. In your country or community, do any children grow up in a home with just one parent?
2. How common do you think this is in the United States?
3. Did your grandparents live with you when you were growing up?
4. Is this common in your community?
5. Do adult children usually live with their parents in your community?

Reading 2

THE FAMILY TODAY

The traditional image of the average family in the United States is of a mother taking care of her two kids and a house in the suburbs while the father drives off to work. In fact, this kind of family is relatively rare today, both in the United States and in many other countries. In
5 its place, new forms of the family unit are increasingly common.

Single and unmarried parents

There has been a rise in the number of children growing up in households with just one parent. Globally, between one-quarter and one-third of all families are headed by single parents, mostly by mothers. In the United States, there are about 14 million single-
10 parent families, which is about 9 percent of all families. The figure in Australia is 14 percent; in the United Kingdom, it is 25 percent. In many developing countries, the percentages are much higher.

Compared with two-parent families, single-parent families usually have lower incomes. They are also more likely to experience social and
15 psychological stress, such as unemployment, lack of social support, and children with problems at school. These challenges are not a direct consequence of the absence of a second parent. They result from factors that can also affect two-parent families, for example, poverty and poor living conditions. One factor causing the increase in
20 single-parent families is the rise in the divorce rate around the world. Also, a growing number of financially independent single women have decided to have children on their own.

In general, there has been an increase in the number of never-married women having children. Some of these women raise their
25 children alone, but not all of these births result in single-parent families. Some couples do not marry, but they decide to have a baby anyway. In the United States, in 2009, 40 percent of births were to unmarried women. The rate is higher in western Europe. The percentage of babies born to unmarried women is about 44 percent in
30 the United Kingdom, 50 percent in France, and 55 percent in Sweden. There is increasing acceptance of unmarried parenthood in these countries and many others.

Blended families

Because of the high rates of divorce and remarriage, *blended families* have also become quite common. These result when two people with
35 children from previous marriages get married. About one-third of all Americans are members of some type of blended family. Because women usually win custody (i.e., care and guardianship) of children

in divorce cases, most blended families consist of a woman, her new husband, and her biological children. The new husband often becomes
40 the children's stepfather.

The happiness of blended families depends largely on how well the stepfather gets along with the children. Being a stepfather can be difficult. Stepfathers are likely to have problems with discipline. The children may resent him and refuse to obey him. If a stepfather tells his
45 young stepson that he should not watch television on a school night, the stepson may reply: "My dad lets me. Besides, it's my mom's TV."

Conflicts are most likely with teenagers. Teenagers are trying hard to break free of adult control. They may accept parental discipline only out of love and respect, which they may not have for their stepfathers.
50 During an argument, teenagers may shout at their stepfathers: "You're not my real father!" Although most blended families are relatively free of serious problems, conflict with stepchildren is one of the main reasons that second marriages fail at a higher rate than first marriages.

Nuclear and extended families

A husband and wife and their children are called a *nuclear family*.
55 This is the typical family unit in most Western countries. In many other parts of the world, however, it is more typical for the *extended family* to live together in one household. It may include grandparents, uncles, aunts, and cousins. This is more common in cultures in which marriage is considered a union between two families rather than just
60 two people.

In cultures where the nuclear family is the typical unit, children usually leave home in their early twenties, often before they get married. Frequently, they leave home when they go to college. Recently, there has been a shift in this behavior. Increasingly, young
65 people are moving back to their parents' homes after they graduate from college. Sometimes even older adult children move back in with their parents if they lose their jobs or cannot afford to pay for their own homes. These adults are sometimes called *boomerang children* because they leave home for a while, but
70 then they return. This is one more example of how the structure of families changes as society changes.

Extended families often include people from three or four generations.

1 Reading for main ideas ®

> Understanding main ideas is an important task when reading a college text. Part of this skill is being able to quickly identify the topic of a paragraph.

Look back at the text quickly and write the number of the paragraph that addresses each of the following topics. A match is given as an example.

1. increase in blended families   Paragraph ___

2. teen conflict with stepfathers   Paragraph ___

3. increase in single-parent families   Paragraph ___

4. traditional versus new families   Paragraph _1_

5. increase in unmarried parents   Paragraph ___

6. nuclear versus extended families   Paragraph ___

7. adult children who return home   Paragraph ___

8. challenges of single-parent families   Paragraph ___

9. challenges of stepfathers   Paragraph ___

2 Word families Ⓥ

> One way to figure out the meaning of an unknown word is to look for its relationship with other words in the same word family. Even if you cannot figure out the exact meaning, your understanding can be enough to allow you to read on. For example, in Paragraph 1 of the text, you can get an idea of the meaning of the word *increasingly* by recognizing that it is related to the word *increase*.

A Look at the phrases from the text. Write down at least one other word you know that is related to the underlined word.

1. <u>Globally</u>, between one-quarter and one-third   *globe / global / globalization*
2. <u>psychological</u> stress   *psychologically / psycho*
3. such as <u>unemployment</u>   *unemploy / employment / employer*
4. <u>financially</u> independent   *financial / finance*
5. <u>unmarried</u> women   *unmarried / marital*
6. unmarried <u>parenthood</u>   *parent / parentally*

B Try to figure out the meanings of the underlined words. Use your dictionary to check your answers.

3 Taking notes Ⓐ Ⓦ

When you take notes, it is important not to write down everything. You should only write down the main points and important details or examples. You should also try to abbreviate (shorten) words (e.g., *incr* = increase).

A Look at these notes taken from the subsection "Single and unmarried parents."

- Sg p and unmarr. p. fams
- Bet. 1/3 and 1/4 fams. in wrld
- US 9%, Aust 14%, UK 25%
- Probs: financ. psych. soc.
- reasons for incr – (1) div. rate (2) sg wm. have
  kids (3) unmarr. cples have kids

B Complete these notes taken from the subsection "Blended families."

Staying single
- women get cust.
- US rate _____
- Probs for stepdad: _____
- Teens: _____
- Reas. 2nd marr. fails: _____

C Use the note-taking models in Steps A and B to write your own notes for the subsection "Nuclear and extended families." Write three notes for each paragraph.

4 Answering short-answer questions Ⓐ Ⓦ

One of the best ways to prepare for a short-answer quiz is to make up some questions that you think you will be asked. Short-answer quizzes usually include three types of questions.

- Type 1: direct questions about the data (i.e., the information and ideas in the text) – *who*, *what*, *when*, *where*, and *how* questions.

- Type 2: questions that ask you to look more closely at the data – to find relationships between different parts of the data, for example, to compare and contrast elements or to analyze causes.

- Type 3: questions that ask you to think critically about what you have read – to evaluate or assess the data and to justify your answer. *no one anser*

A Work with a partner. Answer the questions about the "Nuclear and extended families" subsection of the text:

Type 1 1. What is the meaning of *boomerang children*? *but they come back* — *The children who live home for a while*

Type 1 2. Why are young people returning home to live with their families? *They lose their home. jobs* *or cannot afford to pay for their homes.*

Type 3 3. Why do you think the nuclear family unit is more common in some cultures and the extended family unit is more common in others? *Is more common in cultures, in wich married is considered an union between two families Rather then just 2 people*

B With your partner, read each question again and decide if it is Type 1, 2, or 3.

C With your partner, write two or three questions about each of the other two sections in text ("Single and unmarried parents" and "Blended families"). Try to write a variety of different types of questions.

D Exchange your questions with your partner, and answer each other's questions orally.

1 Predicting ®

> It is a good habit to predict the information in a text before you read it. It can motivate you to read the text and help you start thinking about some of the language that you might find there. You can often predict the general content of a text by looking at its title and headings without skimming the rest of the text.

The title of the text on the next page is "How We Learn to Behave," and the headings are:

Sanctions and modeling

Differences across cultures

Without looking at the text, discuss with a partner the type of information you expect to find there. Then, skim the text to check your predictions.

2 Personalizing the topic ®

> Thinking about your personal connection to a topic can help you take in new information about the topic. You should do this while you are reading as well as before you read.

Before reading the text "How We Learn to Behave," discuss with a small group what you would do if you were the parent in each of the situations below.

1. Your five-year-old child hits another child without reason while playing. You have never seen him or her do this before.
2. Every night, your four-year-old child refuses to go to bed.
3. Your 10-year-old child offers to help you clean up the house.
4. Your oldest child, a 16-year-old, has started smoking. You smoke, but do not want your children to smoke.
5. You want your 14-year-old to take care of your younger children when you are at work, but he or she complains, "It's not my job."

Reading 3 PRe-Reading

HOW WE LEARN TO BEHAVE

- A man turns off his cell phone as he enters a movie theater.
- A woman eats her lunch and puts the paper wrapper in a trash can.
- A young man helps an elderly woman who has fallen.

5   Being polite, neat, and helpful are characteristics of a person who is well socialized into U.S. culture. **Socialization** is the process of learning how to behave in the society we live in. Societies must have some organized way of teaching new members what is expected of them and how they should behave. Through socialization, children
10 develop into adults who know how to behave appropriately in their culture.

The task of socialization is performed by several groups and institutions called *socialization agents*. The family, school, and friends are the most important socialization agents. Of these, the family is
15 the most important, especially during the first years of life. How do families and other agents teach children how to behave? Two important ways are by sanctions and by modeling.

Sanctions and modeling

Sanctions are consequences following a behavior that influence whether the behavior will be repeated. *Negative sanctions* are
20 punishments. This means that something bad happens after undesired behavior occurs. If a child says, "Gimme some gum," and the parent says, "No gum until you learn to ask politely" and does not give the child the gum, then the child learns that it is not a good idea to speak this way. If he does, he will not get what he wants. *Positive sanctions*
25 are rewards. In other words, the behavior is followed by something pleasant, or enjoyable. If a child asks a parent, "May I have some gum, please?" and the parent gives the child some gum, the child learns that saying "please" at the end of a request results in getting what he asked for. Parents generally use negative sanctions when their children are
30 disobedient or rude and positive sanctions when they are polite and well behaved.

Modeling is another way that children learn to behave appropriately. Modeling refers to learning by watching the behavior of others – especially parents – and copying that behavior. Modeling influences
35 both positive and negative behavior. For example, children who are respectful to elderly people have probably seen their parents do things such as helping older people onto trains and buses. On the other hand, children whose parents fight all the time are more likely to behave the same way when they become adults.

Socialization the process of learning what to expect and how to behave in the society in which an individual lives

---

Differences across cultures

⁴⁰ It is easy to assume that every culture socializes children in the same way. Research studies, however, show that there are cross-cultural differences in what families expect of their children and in how they socialize them to behave appropriately. For example, in some Asian families the needs of the group are traditionally ⁴⁵ seen as more important than the needs of the individual. Children learn that their first responsibility is to their parents rather than to themselves. For example, many children work hard at school so that their parents <u>will be proud of them</u>.

There are also differences in the amount of responsibility ⁵⁰ children are expected to take within their families, and this has an important effect on their behavior. A study of six- to eleven-year-old children in six communities in the United States, Kenya, Japan, India, the Philippines, and Mexico revealed a considerable <u>difference</u> across these cultures in the level of responsibility children had. The children ⁵⁵ in Kenya and Mexico were expected to take care of the other younger children in the family and do household chores that helped the whole family. These children quickly learned to be responsible and caring toward others. Parental expectations about work around the house were an important part of children's socialization. In contrast, in the ⁶⁰ United States, children had fewer chores, and they were less likely to develop these traits at an early age. All of these forms of socialization determine how we behave when we become adults.

Parents expect children to help with household chores.

caption

"Tiger Mother"

Socialization of children often remains an important part of a culture even when the group's circumstances change. For example, in many Asian-American homes, the importance of hard work, achievement, and respect for family still plays a key role in socialization of children. In 2010, Amy Chua, a Chinese-American, shocked many American readers when she described

Amy Chua

the way she raised her two daughters. She calls herself a "Tiger Mother." She was very strict with them. She didn't let them watch television or go to their friends' houses to play. She forced one of her daughters to do 2,000 math problems every night until she was the best in the class. She said she would burn her daughter's dolls if she did not play her music perfectly. Her daughters are top students and have won many musical competitions.

1 Reading boxed texts ®

Many academic textbooks include boxed texts. Their purpose varies. They can do the following:

- give an interesting example of an idea in the main text
- give some detailed statistics
- give a definition
- ask you to apply ideas to your own life

Whatever the purpose, these boxed texts usually contain high-interest material that will add to your understanding of the main text.

A Read the boxed section at the end of this text again.

B Discuss its purpose with a small group. Does it match one of the purposes mentioned above?

2 Definitions Ⓦ Ⓥ

Textbooks contain many definitions of words or expressions that have a special meaning within the field of study. These words or expressions are sometimes called *technical terms.* Understanding the structure of these definitions will make it easier to recognize them in texts and help you learn to define the terms you use in writing assignments.

A Read the examples from "How We Learn to Behave." Circle the term being defined and underline the words that link the term and its meaning. The first item is done as an example

1. Socialization is the process of learning how to behave in the society we live in.

2. Sanctions are consequences following a behavior that influence whether the behavior will be repeated.

3. Positive sanctions are rewards. In other words, the behavior is followed by something pleasant or enjoyable.

4. Negative sanctions are punishments. This means that something bad happens after a behavior occurs.

5. Modeling refers to learning by watching the behavior of others – especially parents – and copying that behavior.

B Work with a partner. Discuss the meanings of these words from the text and write a one-sentence definition for each using some of the patterns in the sentences above.

socialization agents (Line 13) _____

negative behavior (Line 35) _____

household chores (Line 56) _____

cross-cultural differences (Lines 41–42) _____

3 Words related to the topic

> It is usually easier to remember words if we learn them as part of a group of related words. So after you read, it is a good idea to look for words that you can group together.

A These words from the text describe different kinds of behavior: *polite*, *neat*, *well behaved*, *disobedient*, *respectful*, *responsible*, *rude*, *caring*.

Work with a partner. Write the words in the chart to show which kinds of behaviors are likely to lead to a positive sanction (a reward) and which to a negative sanction (a punishment). Use the context of the word in the text and a dictionary if necessary.

Positive sanction	Negative sanction
polite	disobedient

B Add these other kinds of behaviors to the chart: *kind*, *impolite*, *cheerful*, *aggressive*, *thoughtful*, *rebellious*, *selfish*, *mean*.

4 Applying what you have read

> Finding ways to apply new knowledge is a good way to deepen your understanding of new subject matter.

A Read the following letters to a magazine advice column and discuss with your classmates what you would advise the parent to do.

- Would you advise a positive sanction?
- Would you advise a negative sanction?
- Do you think some behavior modeling might help, or do you have some other idea?

Letter 1

My eight-year-old son has never been in any trouble before, but just recently he has been getting into big trouble for swearing at school. I'm not sure what to do. My husband and I don't swear very much around the house, but of course, like many people, we do sometimes. My son is usually quite well behaved, but he does not seem to take any notice of what I say about this. What should I do?

Letter 2

My six-year-old daughter has been coming home with small toys that do not belong to her. When I ask her about them, she says that another child gave them to her. But it happens so much that I just cannot believe her. I feel I should punish her in some way, but I 'm not sure if it would work and if it could even make the problem worse. What should I do?

Letter 3

I have four children. The youngest child, a three-year-old boy, has a terrible habit of throwing things at people who visit the house. Because people usually laugh at him when he does this, he thinks his behavior is amusing and keeps doing it. Although people are at first polite, eventually they get upset. It is very embarrassing, and I really don't know what to do. Can you help me?

B Choose one letter and write a short letter of advice in reply.

Chapter 1 Academic Vocabulary Review

The following words appear in the readings in Chapter 1. They all come from the Academic Word List, a list of words that researchers have discovered occur frequently in many different types of academic texts. For a complete list of all the Academic Word List words in this chapter and in all the readings in this book, see the Appendix on pages 213–214.

Reading 1 Marriage: A Changing Institution	Reading 2 The Family Today	Reading 3 How We Learn to Behave
adapt community eventually experts immigrate variation	affect conflict (n) consist couples image incomes	appropriately assume circumstances negative positive task

Complete the sentences with words from the lists.

1. Some _____ wait until they have saved enough money before they marry.

2. People with higher _____ can buy more things, but they are not always happier than people with less money.

3. People who are following norms behave _____ in most situations.

4. _____ give several different reasons for why the age of first marriage has risen in the last 50 years.

5. It is important not to _____ that you know other people's opinions before you ask them.

6. In the past, many people had a _____ opinion about women who did not marry. Today, this has changed, and more women are choosing to remain single.

7. People often choose to _____ to another country for economic and political reasons.

8. Blended families can create _____ among family members until everyone adjusts to the new arrangement.

9. Learning to write in a new language is a difficult _____ .

10. New immigrants must learn to _____ to the customs of their new countries.

11. If you work hard and are patient, _____ you will reach your goals.

12. There is _____ in family structure across different countries and cultures. Families are not the same everywhere.

Developing Writing Skills

In this section you will learn about body paragraphs, which are at the heart of any piece of writing. You will write one body paragraph here. You will also use what you learn here to complete the writing assignment at the end of this unit.

Writing a Body Paragraph

Each body paragraph should be organized around one idea, and everything in the paragraph should be related to that idea. Every body paragraph you write should have a topic sentence. A topic sentence does several things.

- It states the topic of the paragraph, or what the paragraph will be about.
- It makes a claim about the topic. This means that it has to say something important about the topic that is more than a simple fact. The topic sentence makes a claim that you will need to prove.
- It restricts what the other sentences in the paragraph can be about.

A Review the sentences below with a classmate. Decide which ones would make effective topic sentences. If you decide one is not a good topic sentence, explain why.

1. Arranged marriages are often successful.
2. I got married when I was very young.
3. The divorce rate in India doubled last year.
4. There are several reasons for the increase in blended families.
5. Modeling is a better way to socialize children than punishment.

B The topic sentence is often, but not always, the first sentence in the paragraph. As you continue to write your body paragraph, imagine someone has read your topic sentence. Then the reader turns to you and says, "Really? Is that so? Can you prove it to me?" Now ask yourself, does the rest of my paragraph prove it?

The rest of the paragraph must

- relate to the idea stated in the topic sentence
- provide evidence for the claim in the topic sentence

In other words, the other sentences in the paragraph should support the idea in the topic sentence.

Think about the topic sentences that you chose in Step A. For each one, write one other sentence that could be in the paragraph. The sentence should support, or provide evidence for, the claim in the topic sentence.

_____

_____

_____

C Read each sentence in the sample paragraph. Highlight the topic sentence. Then, for each of the sentences in the rest of the paragraph, decide if it is related to the idea in the topic sentence and provides support for its claim. If it does not, cross it out.

> *Arranged marriages are often more successful than "love" marriages. When young people fall in love, they may make quick and unwise decisions. When parents arrange a marriage for their child, they consider for a long time and bring all of their wisdom and experience to the decision. Often they know what will work better in the long run. Their children should be grateful for their help. In India, 95 percent of all marriages are arranged. The divorce rate there has doubled in the last five years. Statistics show that the divorce rate for "love" marriages is much higher than the rate for arranged marriages.*

D Now write a body paragraph. The topic is "sanctions as a form of socialization in your country or your family." Choose one of these to write about:

- Do parents in your country use mostly negative or positive sanctions to teach children how to behave? Do you think they are effective?
- Did your parents use mostly negative or positive sanctions to teach you how to behave? Do you think they are effective?

Begin with your topic sentence. Then write three or four more sentences with examples to support the claim in your topic sentence.

E Proofread your paragraph and make sure there are no grammar, spelling, or punctuation errors.

Chapter 2
The Power of the Group

PREPARING TO READ

Thinking about the topic ®

> In the text "The Influence of Culture" you will read about social norms, or rules. These norms define what acceptable behavior in a society or group is.

A Use the rating scale of 1–4 to indicate how acceptable the following behaviors are in your country or community. Check (✓) one box for each behavior:

1 = completely acceptable

2 = sometimes acceptable

3 = usually unacceptable

4 = completely unacceptable   *dirt looks*

Behavior	1	2	3	4
Sitting on a crowded bus when an elderly person is standing				☑
Eating with your fingers		☑		
Wearing shorts on a main street in your town				☑
Kissing your boyfriend or girlfriend in public	☑			
Hitting a child when he or she misbehaves		☑		
Wearing shoes inside the house		☑		
Swearing in public		☑		
Taking a dog into a restaurant		☑		
Accepting a gift when you have nothing to give in return		☑		
Blowing your nose at the dinner table				☑

B If there are students from different countries in your class, move around the class and talk to other students until you find at least one country that is different from your own for several behaviors. If you all come from the same country, discuss how people's attitudes vary depending on their age, their family background, location, and so on.

C Discuss the following question with your classmates:

What happens in your country if you violate the rules for these behaviors?

Reading 1

THE INFLUENCE OF CULTURE

Imagine that you are alone with a person whom you love and who loves you. You are holding his or her face in your hands as you look into his
5 or her eyes and then you kiss. You probably think of kissing as natural. To a sociologist, kissing and many other common behaviors are *cultural* rather than *natural*. We are not born with the
10 knowledge of how to kiss and what it means to kiss. Instead, we learn this as part of our culture.

The meaning of culture

Culture is a very powerful force in our lives. It determines many of the experiences we have and the meanings we give to them. But what
15 exactly is culture? To the sociologist, culture is everything that we are socialized to do, think, use, and make. We learn much of what we think and do from the society that we live in. Because humans live in groups and communicate with each other, they pass on what they know and believe to each other and to their children.

20 For example, they pass on ideas about what is important in life, what normal and abnormal behavior is, and what is right and wrong. All these ideas are the foundation of the culture of their society, and they guide the behavior of the members of that society.

Values and norms

Values are socially shared ideas about what we consider to be good,
25 desirable, or important in life. We show what we value by how we live our lives and how we view others. For example, if in our society we value professional success, we are likely to spend a lot of time thinking or worrying about it. We respect others who have achieved success, and we teach our children that is it important to be successful. These
30 shared values of a society form the basis of *norms*, which are a set of social rules that most people in the society follow.

Norms define what is socially acceptable or unacceptable behavior in particular social situations. If we violate, or go against, social norms, there will probably be negative consequences. That is, there
35 may be a penalty or punishment to discourage us from acting this way again. Most of us are not even aware that many rules for behavior are social norms. We think they are natural. Rules for kissing are a good example. We know whom we can kiss, how we can kiss, and when

culture everything humans are socialized to do, think, use, and make

[handwritten notes:]

▷ Spanking
↓
Slap on the

▷ Swering
↓
bad word

1 Cultural behavior vs natural
2 Socialization throught culture
3 Culture guides behavior
4 Values are what a culture thinks is important
5 Norms are what is acceptable (weak social rules)
6 Mores are stronger social norms (usually laws)
7 Diffirence in values/norms across cuture
8 values and norms can, but don't always change over time.

and where. Norms like these are relatively weak, so the consequences for violating them are not very serious. These are sometimes called *folkways*. Folkways are customs that members of a group are expected to follow to show courtesy to others. For example, saying "excuse me" when you burp is an American folkway. Thanking someone if they say you have done a job well is another. If you violate these weak norms, nobody will punish you. Someone might think you are strange or impolite, but that is all.

Mores are much stronger social norms. They provide the standards of moral behavior for a group or society. Violation of mores can carry a severe penalty. In modern societies, most mores are formalized as *laws*. The government enforces laws. Thus, violations of these mores are considered *crimes*. For example, parents must care for their children. In the United States and many other countries, there are laws that allow the government to take children away from parents who do not take care of them properly. There are also laws in many countries that very strongly encourage people to drive safely by having penalties for driving too fast.

Differences in values and norms

Values and norms vary from culture to culture. As a result, some norms and their underlying values may be considered important in one society but not in another. If someone says to you, "Good job!" an American norm tells you to respond, "Thank you." This is because of the value Americans place on a fair exchange – praise for good work. In China, however, the same praise would receive a humbler response such as, "Oh, no, I have done poorly." This is because humility ranks high in the Chinese value system. This kind of difference in values and norms can sometimes lead to *cross-cultural misunderstandings*.

Throwing rice is an old custom that can still be seen at weddings today.

Both values and norms may change with time. However, norms for behavior sometimes persist even after their underlying values have changed. For example, many people throw rice at weddings. Rice is a symbol of fertility, a quality that was highly valued by society in the past. Today, we are no longer very concerned about the number of children a couple will have, yet we continue to throw rice at weddings.

1 Reading actively ®

Academic textbooks contain extensive explanations of fundamental concepts in a particular field as well as many field-specific definitions. As a result, it is often possible to understand the structure of these texts in terms of *Wh-* questions (What? Who? When? Where? How?). Creating a list of *Wh-* questions can help you remember the information in the text and prepare for tests.

Read the *Wh-* questions. Match them to the appropriate paragraph number. Write the paragraph number in the blank before each question. Start with the second paragraph.

___ **a.** What are mores?

___ **b.** How do values vary across time?

___ **c.** What are values?

___ **d.** How do values vary across cultures?

___ **e.** What is culture?

___ **f.** What are norms?

2 Understanding key terms ® Ⓥ

Your understanding of the texts you read depends in part on your understanding of key terms. Pay careful attention to the explanations of these terms and any examples used in the text to help you understand them.

Find explanations and examples in the text of the following terms. Complete the chart using note form.

Term	Explanation	Examples
Values	shared ideas about what is good & right	humility
Norms		
Folkways		
Mores		
Laws		
Crimes		

3 Expanded definitions Ⓦ Ⓡ

A Use the information from the chart in Task 2 to write expanded definitions. When you write a definition, it can help your reader if you expand it by giving one or two examples.

Below is an expanded definition of culture. It begins by defining the term but then adds some information about kissing, a culturally learned behavior.

Culture is everything we are socialized to do, think, use, and make. Kissing, for example, is a cultural rather than a natural behavior. We kiss because we have learned this behavior from others in our cultural group.

B Look back at the text and at the notes you completed for Task 2, and write a one-sentence definition of two of the key terms.

C Now add two examples of the term to help a reader understand it. Don't use the examples in the text. Use examples from your own experience of a society you know and understand.

4 Collocations Ⓥ

When you read in English, you will notice that some words often appear together. For example, *goal* often appears with *reach*, and *chance* with *slight.* These word combinations are called *collocations.* It is important to learn these word combinations. They will help you read more quickly and write more natural English.

A The nouns on the list appear in the text. Find the verbs and adjectives that appear with them to make a collocation. The chart indicates (with •) whether the collocation is with a verb or adjective or both. Fill in the chart with the appropriate word from the text.

	Collocation with Adjective	Collocation with Verb
force (Line 13)	•	
behavior (Lines 21, 48)	•	
success (Line 28)		•
norms (Line 33)		•
consequences (Line 34)	•	
courtesy (Line 42)		•
penalty (Line 49)	•	
laws (Line 50)		•

B Use your knowledge of collocations from Step A to complete the following sentences.

1. If you work hard, you will achieve _____ in your career.

2. It is important to show _____ to others even when you are angry.

3. There is a severe _____ for drunk driving.

4. In most communities, the police have the power to enforce _____ .

5. If you violate _____ in your community, there may be a penalty.

6. Abnormal _____ is activity that society thinks is strange or unusual.

7. Parents are a powerful _____ in their children's lives.

8. Stealing a police car carries a more severe _____ than stealing an ordinary car.

9. There are negative _____ for violating society's norms.

1 Personalizing the topic ®

A Work with two or three other students. Think back to when you were 14 or 15 years old and discuss:

1. What did you like to wear?
2. What type of music did you like?
3. Who were your favorite singers, TV and film stars, and sports stars?
4. What did you do in your free time?
5. What did your parents think about your interests and your sense of fashion?

B Still working in the same groups, discuss teenagers now:

1. What clothes do they like to wear?
2. What types of music do they like?
3. Who are some singers, TV and film stars, or sports stars who are popular with teenagers?
4. What are some activities that many teenagers participate in?
5. What do you think about these teenage interests and fashion?
6. If you are not a teenager, in what ways are these different from when you were their age?

2 Previewing art ®

> Looking at the photographs or at other art in a text and reading the captions (the words that explain visual materials) is a good way to get an overview of the content.

A Look at the photographs in the text "Peer Groups" and read the captions. Write a sentence to describe what you think the text will be about.

B Compare sentences with others in the class. After you have read the text, return to your group's sentence to see whose sentence was the most accurate.

Reading 2

PEER GROUPS

During **adolescence**, people become increasingly involved with their *peer group*, a group whose members are about the same age and have similar interests. The peer group – along with the family and the school – is one of the three main agents of socialization. However, the
5 peer group is very different from the family and the school. Whereas parents and teachers have more power than children and students, the peer group is made up of equals.

Learning from the peer group

Peer groups develop among all age groups, but they are particularly important for adolescents' development. The adolescent peer group
10 teaches its members several important things. First, it teaches social skills – how to get along with other people. Second, the peer group teaches its members the values of friendship among equals. Third, and perhaps most important, it teaches them to be independent from adult authorities. Sometimes this means that a peer group encourages
15 its members to go against authorities and adults – to ignore home and school rules and even to break the law. Most teenagers, though, rebel only by making fun of older people in a harmless way.

These traits are typical of adolescents in modern, Western societies, but it is important to remember that this kind of rebellious behavior
20 is partly cultural and it is not universal. Adolescence is actually a relatively new concept. One hundred years ago, teenagers were expected to work and help their families. In other words, they had to act like adults; there was no time for adolescence. In
25 addition, the role that the peer group plays in helping adolescents break away from adult authority is based on fundamental Western values of individualism and independence. There may be differences
30 across cultures in how adolescents behave. They may depend less on their peer group and they may not seek independence from their families.

Peer groups often develop subcultures
35 with their own distinct values, language, music, dress, and heroes. Members of these groups often believe in the same things, talk the same way, dress the same way, listen to the same music, and like and dislike the
40 same celebrities.

adolescence
the period between childhood and adulthood

Peer groups often have their own values and styles.

Adolescent peer groups frequently differ from parents and teachers in what they value. Whereas parents and teachers tend to place great importance on success in school and careers, adolescent peer groups are likely to think that popularity, social leadership, and athletic
45 achievement are more important. These differences do not necessarily mean that parents and teenagers always fight and argue. They simply engage in different types of activities – work and task activities with parents, but social activities and recreation with peers. They are inclined to seek advice from parents on financial, educational, career,
50 and other serious matters. With their peers, they are more likely to discuss social activities such as which boy or girl to date and what clubs to join.

Negative peer pressure

Peer group members often look to each other for approval instead of relying on their own personal beliefs. Doing what everyone else
55 is doing is more important than being independent and individual. Although young people can learn valuable lessons from peers, sometimes the pressure from peers can also have a negative effect. First, peers may pressure members of the group to do things that they know are wrong or dangerous. Second, strong *peer group conformity*
60 may result in *ingroups* and *outgroups*. Ingroups have common interests and shared attitudes, but they also may try to exclude those who have different interests or beliefs or who behave differently. These groups are sometimes called *cliques*. People who are excluded from these cliques are in outgroups. Unfortunately, sometimes individuals in
65 outgroups receive strong negative attention, called *bullying*. Bullying may be continuous teasing, but it may become more serious and include **harassment** and physical **abuse** as well. All kinds of bullying are harmful.

As young people grow into middle and late adolescence, usually
70 their involvement with peers gradually declines because of their growing independence. As they reach the end of their adolescence, they tend to adopt more adult values, such as wanting to get good grades and good jobs. The power of the group begins to decrease.

harassment
behavior that continuously annoys or troubles another person

abuse cruel treatment

Cliques may exclude people from their groups.

1 Reviewing for a test Ⓐ Ⓡ

> Reviewing the text with a classmate can deepen your understanding of the material and help you prepare for a test. Connecting material to your own experience can help you to remember what you have read.

A Work with a partner. Without looking back at the text, discuss the answers to the following questions. Use what you remember from the text and your own experiences.

1. Name two important things the adolescent peer group teaches young people.
2. Adolescent rebellion is often encouraged by the peer group. Has this always been true of adolescents? Explain why or why not. Is it true in all cultures? Explain why or why not.
3. Name a topic that adolescents are likely to discuss with their parents. Was this true for you?
4. Name a topic that they are likely to discuss with their peers. Was this true for you?
5. In what ways can peer groups have a negative influence?

B Now look back at the text and check your answers.

2 Synonyms Ⓥ

> Textbook writers often have to refer many times to one thing (e.g., an idea, an event, a group of people) in the same chapter or reading. To avoid repeating the same words over and over, they often choose different words to express the same idea. When you write, you should do the same thing. Try to vary your language and use words that are less common.

A The words in the list below are quite common. There are words in the text that have a similar meaning but are less common. Find them and write them on the lines below.

1. idea (Par. 3) _____
2. basic (Par. 3) _____
3. different, separate (Par. 4) _____
4. success (Par. 5) _____
5. likely to (Par. 5) _____
6. look for (Par. 5) _____
7. economic (Par. 5) _____
8. depend (Par. 6) _____
9. keep out (Par. 6) _____
10. decrease (Par. 7) _____

B Read the sentences with the boldfaced words. Then decide which is a more likely conclusion, *a* or *b*.

1. The girls **excluded** the little boy from their games.
   a. He was mad.
   b. He was happy.

2. The country had **economic** problems.
   a. There are many new factories.
   b. There are many poor people.

3. After his interview on Monday, he was **inclined to** take the job in California.
   a. On Tuesday, he decided to stay at his old job.
   b. On Tuesday, he accepted the job in California.

4. The number of jobs in the country **declined** significantly in 2012.
   a. The government reported the good news.
   b. The government is very concerned.

5. The new student just did not understand the **concepts** in physics.
   a. The calculations were very difficult.
   b. The theories were unfamiliar.

6. The police said they are **seeking** a tall bald man with a beard.
   a. They are keeping this man in prison.
   b. They want to find this man so they can talk to him.

7. Western culture places a high value on **achievement**.
   a. In the West, rich people get a lot of respect.
   b. In the West, religious leaders are very important.

8. The designer from Japan has a very **distinct** style.
   a. His clothes are simple and comfortable.
   b. His clothes are not like anything we have seen before.

9. There are **fundamental** differences between Eastern and Western culture.
   a. People are really the same everywhere.
   b. There are often cross-cultural misunderstandings.

10. She could not **rely on** her family.
    a. Her family had no money.
    b. She had no money to give her family.

3 Describing differences Ⓦ Ⓡ

A Study the four different sentence structures from the text that express the differences between the peer group and other socializing agents:

1. X *is different from* Y
However, the peer group is very different **from** the family and the school. (Par. 1)

2. *Whereas* X + *verb . . .* Y + *verb . . . .*
Whereas parents and teachers **have** more power than children and students, the peer group **is** made up of equals. (Par. 1)

3. *There is a difference + preposition . . .*
There may be differences **across** cultures in how adolescents behave. (Par. 3)

4. X *differ(s) from* Y
Adolescent peer groups frequently differ from parents and teachers . . . (Par. 5)

B Read the paragraph below that describes one difference between adolescents and adults. Find examples of the four sentence structures in the paragraph and circle them. One is done for you as an example.

(Teenagers differ from adults) *in the way they handle finances. Teenagers are likely to spend all their money as soon as they receive it whereas most adults try to save some of their money for future expenses. There is also a difference in what adults and adolescents spend their money on. Whereas older people are more likely to spend their money on the things they need – clothes, food, housing – young people tend to spend it on the things they want – music, movies, going out.*

C Write a paragraph describing another area of difference between adolescents and adults (e.g., clothes, friendships, interests). Use the sentence patterns above and vary the way you refer to the two groups.

1 Thinking about the topic ®

Look at the news photos and captions and discuss these questions with your classmates:

1. What is similar about the scenes in these photographs?
2. What is different?
3. Have you ever been in situations like these?

Passersby stop to watch a street performer.

Protests erupted about pollution during an international environmental conference

A protester is taken away by police during a peaceful protest

2 Skimming ®

> Reading the first sentence of each paragraph is a good way of getting an overview of what a text is about. The first sentence of a paragraph is often its topic sentence: the sentence that introduces the content of the whole paragraph.

Read the first sentence of each paragraph in the text. Then work with a partner to find the paragraphs that do the following things. Write the paragraph numbers next to the things they do.

a. ___ defines the term *collective behavior*

b. ___ explains one reason why crowds act the way they do

c. ___ asks you to think about your own "crowd" experiences

d. ___ explains some negative consequences of crowd behavior

e. ___ defines the term *crowd*

 f. ___ explains problems with the original theory of crowd behavior

g. ___ explains some characteristics of crowds

Reading 3

CROWDS

The power of the group is important for peers and friends, but it can also have an impact on total strangers. Have you ever had an experience like either of these?

- You are at a football game. Some people in the crowd stand up and
5   wave their arms in the air. Another group of people does the same thing. Soon, you are standing up and doing it, too. Finally, the whole stadium is involved in the action and the excitement of the "wave."

- You are walking along the street on your way to work or school when you see a crowd on the corner. Although you are in a hurry, you
10   walk toward it. You discover that the crowd is watching a man selling gold and silver watches. He is a good salesman and, even though the watches are not cheap, many people are lining up to buy them.

Actions by crowds are one example of what sociologists call *collective behavior*. Collective behavior is social behavior that is
15 relatively unorganized, spontaneous, and unpredictable. It contrasts with *institutional behavior*, which occurs in a well-organized, rather predictable way. Institutional behavior is frequent and regular; for example, every weekday, masses of people hurry to work. At every university, groups of students walk to classes. These predictable
20 patterns are controlled by social norms and are essential for social order. We could not survive without them. Collective behavior, however, is unpredictable and occurs outside these norms.

Crowds and emotion

So what exactly is a crowd? A crowd is a group of people temporarily doing something while they are physically close to one another. They
25 may be gathered on a street corner watching a salesman or at a stadium watching a football game. They may be on a street, throwing things at police, or they may be at a rock concert or a religious meeting. Many psychologists believe there are three basic human emotions: joy, anger, and fear. Collective behavior in a crowd can be categorized according
30 to these emotions. A crowd at a rock concert may act together in joy and excitement. In contrast, a group of people who have gathered to protest a government action may express their anger. A group of people running away from people who are shooting at them will act in fear.

Sometimes emotional crowd behavior can lead to tragedy. A hostile
35 crowd may turn violent, throwing rocks and breaking windows. Fear in a crowd may lead to panic, that is, a sudden and irrational fear. In 1990 in Mecca, Saudi Arabia, thousands of Muslim pilgrims were

walking through a very long tunnel when the lights accidentally went out. The people were frightened and started a *stampede*. They pushed
40 their way through the tunnel, sometimes stepping on other people in their path. 1,426 people died. A frightened crowd at a festival caused a similar stampede on a bridge in Cambodia in 2010. More than 300 people died in that tragedy.

Explanations for crowd behavior

Nearly all crowds share a few traits. First, the individuals in the
45 crowd do not share a clear idea about how to behave or about what will happen. Another characteristic is that a feeling, attitude, or idea spreads very quickly among members of a crowd. Crowd members also tend to follow the actions of others without thinking too much about them. Finally, people in a crowd tend to say and do things they
50 would not normally say and do.

One theory to explain why crowds seem to act collectively is Gustave Le Bon's *social contagion theory*. Le Bon believed that the large number of people in a crowd allows our primitive side to emerge. His theory was that we normally hide this primitive side behind a "mask"

Stampedes often lead to tragedy.

55 of civilized behavior. When we are in a crowd, the large numbers give us a different kind of mask. In a crowd we are faceless and nameless, and this allows us to act in an emotional and irrational way. We would probably never behave this way in our normal, civilized lives.

Today most sociologists think this explanation is too simple. It 60 only seems that everyone in a crowd is acting in the same way, but they probably are not. A different perspective is found in the *emergent-norm theory*. This theory says that members of a crowd develop a new norm to guide their behavior in a particular situation. Although not everyone might agree about what to do, there is great social pressure 65 to behave like other members of the crowd. For example, not everyone in the football crowd feels comfortable about taking part in the wave, but they feel that they have to do it because everyone else is doing it. Sometimes, people may be in crowds where dangerous or *antisocial behavior* becomes the norm – fighting, pushing, or burning cars, for 70 example. Again, not every person in these crowds is likely to follow these behaviors or think they are a good idea, but the crowd has a power of its own.

Hooliganism

Hooliganism is a form of collective behavior that sometimes occurs at or after sports events. It includes destructive and often violent activities by fans of opposing teams. Examples range from angry shouting to fights among hundreds of fans with bottles, stones, and even knives. In some cases, the fights have caused panic in a crowd, causing walls or fences to collapse. In 1985, at the European Cup final in Brussels, 39 people died when Belgian and English soccer fans rioted and a wall in the stadium collapsed on them.

1 Understanding text structure Ⓦ Ⓡ

An academic text may have recurring patterns. After you have seen these patterns several times, you will recognize them and start to predict them. Knowledge of text structure can also help you to prepare for tests because these patterns make it easier to remember information in your readings. Common patterns in academic textbooks include

a. introduction of a new concept or term

b. description or definition

c. familiar example(s)

A Read the excerpt from the text below. Mark the sections of the excerpt to show Parts a, b, and c.

. . . **institutional behavior**, which occurs in a well-organized, rather predictable way. Institutional behavior is frequent and regular. For example, every weekday, masses of people hurry to work.

B Read through the section of the text called "Crowds and emotion" and find the following terms. Mark the text to show Parts a, b, and c.

- crowd
- panic
- stampede

C Read the section of the text called "Explanations for crowd behavior." Find another term that follows this pattern.

D Write about another concept or term that you know about. Use the same text structure.

2 Applying what you have read ⓡ

> Finding ways to apply new knowledge is a good way to deepen your understanding of new subject matter.

A Think of one crowd situation you have been in. How does it relate to the five crowd characteristics described in the text? Complete the checklist.

	Yes	No	Not sure
Did you or other members of the crowd seem uncertain about how to behave and about what would happen?			
Did you or other members of the crowd feel that something had to be done right away to solve a common problem?			
Did a feeling, an attitude, or an idea spread very quickly among crowd members?			
Did you or other members of the crowd go along easily with the actions of others?			
Did members of the crowd say and do things they might not normally say and do? Did you?			

B Discuss your checklist with a partner. Begin by describing the crowd scene – where and when it occurred and who was involved.

C Discuss the following question with your classmates:

Which of the two theories given in the text – emergent-norm or social contagion – do you think offers a better explanation of crowd behavior? Give examples from your experience to support your view.

3 Using grammar to guess meaning ⓥ ⓡ

> An important part of figuring out the meaning of a new word is recognizing it as a noun, a verb, an adjective, an adverb, or another part of speech. You may already know a related word that is a different part of speech. This can help you narrow down possible meanings for the new word and understand any context clues.

A Work with a partner. Find these words in the text and decide whether they are nouns, verbs, adjectives, or adverbs. Then try to guess what they mean.

Word	Part of speech	Related word(s)	Possible meaning
salesman (Line 11)	noun	sale, sell	A person who sells something
unpredictable (Line 15)			
temporarily (Line 23)			
physically (Line 24)			
psychologists (Line 28)			
categorized (Line 29)			
accidentally (Line 38)			
collectively (Line 51)			
faceless (Line 56)			
irrational (Line 57)			
emergent (Line 61)			

B Compare answers with another pair of students.

4 Describing behavior Ⓥ Ⓡ

The reading contains many words that describe how people behave when they are in a crowd.

spontaneous	unpredictable	emotional
predictable	hostile	irrational
antisocial	civilized	

A Find the words from the list above in the text and decide whether they describe behavior that falls within society's norms or behavior that is outside society's norms.

Within norms   **Outside norms**

_____   _____

_____   _____

_____   _____

_____   _____

B Choose the correct adjective in parentheses in the sentences below according to the information in the reading.

1. The behavior of people in an angry crowd is particularly (predictable / unpredictable).

2. Institutional behavior is (rarely spontaneous / often hostile).

3. Burning cars and fighting are examples of (antisocial / irrational) behavior.

4. When people are in a crowd, they sometimes engage in (more civilized / more emotional) behavior than they would when they are alone.

Chapter 2 Academic Vocabulary Review

The following words appear in the readings in Chapter 2. They all come from the Academic Word List, a list of words that researchers have discovered occur frequently in many different types of academic texts. For a complete list of all the Academic Word List words in this chapter and in all the readings in this book, see the Appendix on pages 213–214.

Reading 1 The Influence of Culture	Reading 2 Peer Groups	Reading 3 Crowds
abnormal aware enforce persist professional (adj) violation	attitude authority conformity distinct ignore involve	collapse (v) contrast (v) impact (n) similar theory teams

Complete the following sentences with words from the lists above.

1. The two sisters look very _____ , but they are not twins.
2. We are often not _____ of cultural norms because we are so accustomed to following them.
3. It is important to find a balance between our _____ lives and our personal lives.
4. The police _____ the laws of the city. They arrest people who break laws.
5. The school children were not very nice to the new student. They _____ him and did not include him in their games.
6. Teenagers often rebel against the _____ of their parents. They do not want to follow their parents' rules.
7. Athletic students often play on several different _____ in school, for instance, basketball, football, and tennis.
8. There are many different _____ about the origin of the universe.
9. The pain in his arm _____ for a long time after the accident.
10. A positive _____ is an important element of success.
11. The roof on the old house _____ in the strong wind.
12. The teacher was worried about her student's _____ behavior. She was concerned that he might have psychological problems.

Practicing Academic Writing

In this unit you have learned about the influence of group membership on human behavior and on society. Based on everything you have read and discussed in class, write an essay about this topic.

The Power of the Group

You will write a two-paragraph essay illustrating the power of the group. Think about an influential experience you have had as a member of a group currently or when you were younger. This could be a formal group, such as a high school orchestra, or a more informal peer group.

- Describe the values of the group and its norms for behavior.
- Analyze why it was an influential experience.
- Evaluate whether it was or has been a positive or negative experience.

PREPARING TO WRITE

Planning a text with *Wh-* questions

In Chapter 2, Reading 1, you analyzed the text using *Wh-* questions. In this assignment, you will go in the opposite direction. You will begin with the *Wh-* questions on the left-hand side of the chart to plan an essay of your own. On the right-hand side, make some notes to answer the questions. You will use the notes to write your essay. The sample notes in the third column are examples.

	Wh- question	Sample Notes	Notes
Description	What is the group?	High school science club	
	What is/was its purpose?	Prepare for national science competition	
	What is/was its most important value?	academic success	
	What are/were some norms for behavior?	never boast about your success	
	How are/were new members socialized?	new members had the worst jobs you could only be an officer if you won a prize in a competition	
Influence	What positive lessons did I learn/have I learned?	importance of research	
	What negative experiences did I have/have I had?	Intense pressure	

A Exchange charts with a classmate. Discuss the information on your chart and answer any questions your classmate has.

B Before you start to write, think about how you can connect the general idea of the power of the group with your own particular experience. Review the readings in this chapter, especially the second reading. In your essay, make a claim about the power of group membership based on your readings, and then support the claim with evidence from your own experience in a group. Make notes about important terms in the readings that you may want to use in your essay.

NOW WRITE

Writing first drafts

> Your first piece of writing on a topic is a first draft. Very few people write a "perfect" first draft. A first draft gets some ideas, sentences, and paragraphs down on paper that you can then read through and work out how to improve.

A Review the chart you created in the Preparing to Write section. Decide what claim you want to make about the influence of a group in your past or current experience. Write a sentence that makes this claim.

B Review the writing assignment on body paragraphs at the end of Chapter 1. Begin your essay with one or two sentences that state the impact of groups in general and introduce the specific group you will write about.

C Your essay will have two paragraphs: The first one will provide a **description** (see Column 1 of the chart) of the group and its practices.

- Begin the first paragraph with your sentence(s) from Step A.
- Then write a sentence that makes a claim about the topics you will discuss in the paragraph – values, norms, and socialization. This will be the topic sentence for your paragraph.
- Continue with additional sentences that answer the questions from your chart. The rest of the paragraph should give the reader a full description of the group of which you were/are a member.

The second paragraph will analyze the **influence** the group has/had on you (see Column 1 of your chart).

- Begin with a sentence that makes a claim about the influence this group had on you. This will be the topic sentence of your second paragraph.
- Continue with additional sentences that answer the questions from your chart. The rest of the paragraph should help the reader understand your experience with this group and how it influenced you.

AFTER YOU WRITE

Once you have written a first draft, you can revise and edit it. Revising refers to the process of improving the content of the essay; editing refers to making the language of the essay accurate. You need to consider whether you have responded to the assignment and expressed yourself clearly.

A Read the passages below. With a classmate, discuss which one would make the best beginning for a paragraph like yours and why. Then compare your choice to the sentences that begin your essay.

- I had a very influential experience with a powerful group. My high school science club had a powerful effect on me. The purpose of the club was to prepare us for competitions . . .
- Groups have a powerful influence on individuals. My own experience with my high school science club illustrates this. The purpose of the club was to prepare us for competitions . . .
- The powerful influence of groups is clear from my own experience in high school. The purpose of the club was to prepare us for competitions . . .

B Now reread your own essay. Check that

- The first paragraph has a sentence that connects the general topic of group influence to your experience. Underline it.
- Each body paragraph has a topic sentence. Underline them.
- You have answered the questions from the chart.
- You have used some of the terms from the readings.

If any elements are missing or need to be changed, make notes about the revisions you will make.

C Exchange essays with a partner. Review his or her paper.

- Check for the elements in Step B, above.
- Does the author include facts or examples from his or her own experience or knowledge?

D Revise your essay.

- Review your partner's suggestions.
- Review your own notes for revision.
- Make necessary changes.

E Edit your essay.

- Read through your essay now for possible spelling mistakes, punctuation errors, subject-verb agreement errors, incorrect use of past tense, and article usage.
- Make corrections whenever you find errors.

Unit 2
Gender in Society

In this unit you will look at issues related to being male and being female. In Chapter 3 you will read about some major influences on how we perceive our gender roles and how this affects our behavior. In Chapter 4 you will read about gender issues that affect our lives every day, particularly in the workplace. You will examine ways in which men and women are treated differently.

Contents

In Unit 2, you will read and write about the following topics.

Skills

In Unit 2, you will practice the following skills.

R Reading Skills

Skimming
Personalizing the topic
Examining graphics
Predicting
Reading for main ideas
Applying what you have read
Thinking about the topic
Increasing reading speed
Reading for details
Previewing art

W Writing Skills

Showing contrast
Summarizing
Using adverbs
The passive voice
Pronoun reference
Going beyond the text
Supporting main ideas
Writing an introductory paragraph

V Vocabulary Skills

Cues for finding word meaning
Describing people
Word families
Describing personality and emotion
Guessing meaning from context
Collocations

A Academic Success Skills

Making a chart
Answering short-answer questions
Responding to a quote
Answering definition questions on a test

Learning Outcomes

Write a "Yes, but . . . " essay about whether it is better to be a man or a woman

Previewing the Unit

> Before reading a unit (or chapter) of a textbook, it is a good idea to preview the contents page and think about the topics that will be covered. This will give you an overview of how the unit is organized and what it is going to be about.

Read the contents page for Unit 2 on page 54 and do the following activities.

Chapter 3: Gender Roles

In Chapter 3 you will read about how boys and girls are treated differently when they are small and how some of these differences continue when they go to school. Discuss with a small group:

1. What jobs did you perform around the house when you were growing up? *clean cook*
2. Did you have certain jobs because you were a boy or because you were a girl? *no*
3. At school, were there some subjects or activities that were mostly for boys and other subjects or activities that were mostly for girls? *boys - soccer girls - talking*
4. Were most of your teachers men or women? *50/50*

Chapter 4: Gender Issues Today

In Chapter 4 you will read about some of the challenges that adult men and women have to overcome in their lives.

1. In this survey American men and women were asked to respond to the following statements. The numbers show the percentage of people surveyed who agreed with the statements. Study the results.

	Men	Women
Men have a better life than women.	12%	23%
Being married is very important.	58%	53%
Women can have a good life without marriage.	38%	54%

Source: **Time magazine**

2. Do any of these results surprise you? Discuss your reactions with your classmates.
3. How would you respond to these statements? Discuss your reasons with your classmates.
4. Do you think your parents would respond differently?

Chapter 3
Gender Roles

PREPARING TO READ

1 Skimming ®

Skim the text, taking particular note of the headings, pictures, and their captions.

Which of the following sentences do you think states the main idea of the text?
   a. Boys and girls are usually brought up differently.
   b. It is important for boys and girls to learn their gender roles.
   c. There are good and bad reasons for bringing up girls and boys differently.

2 Personalizing the topic ®

Look at each of the toys and discuss the following questions with a partner:

   1. What is the toy?

   2. Is the toy for boys or girls? Of what age?

   3. Would you buy these toys for children you know? Why or why not?

   4. What kinds of toys did you play with as a child? (e.g., dolls, balls, toy cars)

   5. Do you think the toys you played with influenced you as an adult in any way?

Reading 1

GROWING UP MALE OR FEMALE

Newborn babies do not know if they are boys or girls, but it does not take them long to find out. They very quickly learn the way that their society expects males and females to behave and think. That is, they learn their gender roles.

Children and gender roles

5 From the moment of birth, babies are usually treated according to their gender. In the United States and in many western countries, baby girls tend to be dressed in pink clothing and baby boys in blue. Baby girls are handled more gently than boys. Girls are cuddled and kissed while boys are more frequently bounced around and lifted high in the
10 air. Girls are often given dolls whereas boys are given cars, trucks, and building blocks. Mothers think about how pretty their little girls look but are less concerned about their little boys' appearance.

Parents socialize boys and girls differently. Socialization is the process of transferring values and standards of behavior to new
15 members of a group so that they can fit into society. There are differences in the way parents talk to their children. Parents use words about feelings and emotions more with girls than with boys, and, by age two, girls use these words more than boys do. Furthermore, mothers and fathers talk differently because of their own socialization
20 experiences. Mothers tend to talk more politely. They may say, "Could you turn off the TV, please?" whereas fathers tend to use more direct language, "Turn off the TV." By age four, girls and boys have learned to imitate these conversational styles.

Little girls are generally socialized to be ladylike – polite and quiet. They are taught to rely on others – especially males – for help. They are allowed to express their emotions more freely. Girls learn the importance of being pretty. They may even learn that they must rely more on their beauty than on their intelligence. In contrast, boys are taught to behave "like men." Boys are also encouraged to be independent and strong and to avoid being "mama's boys." They are told that boys don't cry. As a result, boys may grow up with a fear of being feminine and, as young men, try to keep up a macho, that is, very masculine, image.

Growing into gender roles

Socialization into gender roles continues as children grow up and learn from their peers. Boys play rough games with their friends. They are physical and competitive in their play. Parents and teachers often accept that this is normal for boys. Boys who do not engage in this kind of behavior are often teased. Boys' friendships are often based on physical ability and dominant behavior. Girls, on the other hand, tend to play more quietly in smaller groups of friends. They have more intense friendships, based on emotional connections and shared secrets. They also focus more on their appearance than boys do and may tease girls who are not attractive.

Parents also have different expectations of daughters and sons as they grow up. Daughters, more than sons, are socialized to think about the family. For example, they are expected to remember birthdays, to spend time with the family on holidays, and, when they get older, to provide care for sick family members and relatives. Sons are not expected to do these things as much.

Sons are often given more freedom than daughters. Parents often expect their sons be more interested in the world outside the family and more independent of the family in social activities than their daughters. Many parents also believe that daughters need more protection than sons. For example, they may require their daughters to come home earlier at night and forbid them to go to places where they might let their sons go. Such protectiveness often discourages girls from being independent and exploring their environment.

Resisting traditional gender roles

gender-neutral
the same for both sexes

From parents, teachers, and their peers, boys and girls learn the gender roles that society expects them to play. Increasingly today, many parents try to bring up their children in a **gender-neutral** way. They encourage their sons to express their feelings. They encourage their daughters to be independent. However, parents may find it difficult to bring up their children in a gender-neutral way. They are continually fighting against the gender lessons of television, books, peers, and school.

cuddle – cariñoso

1 Making a chart Ⓐ Ⓦ

It can be useful to make a chart (or table) when taking notes, especially when the text compares and contrasts two or more ideas. You can use these charts when you study for a test.

A Look back at the text and complete the chart below with information about the different ways boys and girls are brought up.

	Girls	Boys
Color of clothing	**pink**	blue
Ways children are handled	more gently	less gently
Toys	dolls make-up	**trucks**
Attention to appearance	cute soft pretty	Tough posh less concern
Language	more polite emotional	oposite rude
Expected behavior	more with family emocoral soft	more freedom Tough/ strong
Play style	emotional conecto shared secrets.	physical and capetitive
Friendships	dominant, emotion. felling	relax, strong
Treatment by parents	think more in family	more freedom hard

B Look at your chart and discuss with a partner how this chart might be different if it were about bringing up children in your country.

Fact   opinion
3   1 - False fact
4   2
7   5
8   6

2 Showing contrast Ⓦ Ⓡ

A Notice that the linking word (in bold type) in this sentence (Par. 2) introduces a dependent clause (underlined).

Girls are cuddled and kissed **while** <u>boys are more frequently bounced around and lifted high in the air</u>.

Study the common linking words that show contrast. Notice their grammatical features.

	Can begin a sentence	Introduces a main clause	Introduces a dependent clause	Paragraph in text
while	✓		✓	2
whereas	✓		✓	2
but		✓		2
in contrast	✓	✓		4
on the other hand	✓	✓		5
however	✓	✓		8

B Look back at the text and find examples of these linking words. Notice the punctuation that is used with each of them.

C Choose linking words from the chart to complete these sentences. More than one linking word may fit. Pay attention to the punctuation that is used with each one.

1. Adults often talk about girl babies as "sweet," or "pretty." _____ , they speak of boy babies as "handsome," "tough," and "strong."

2. Some parents expect boys to enjoy playing outdoors. _____ , they expect girls to play indoors with dolls.

3. Some modern parents encourage their daughters to play with cars _____ they encourage their sons to play with kitchen toys.

4. Children's books often present stereotyped gender roles. They tend to show women who stay home _____ show men who have adventures.

5. _____ teachers accept rough, physical actions from boys, they may not accept similar behavior from girls.

6. Some parents try to raise their children in a gender-neutral way, _____ society may reinforce traditional gender roles.

D Use the information in the "Making a Chart" task to write two sentences that describe the contrast between growing up as a girl and growing up as a boy. Use linking words and correct punctuation in your sentences.

3 Cues for finding word meaning V R

Textbooks often include words that are unfamiliar but are important for understanding the material. Sometimes you will have to look them up in a dictionary, but sometimes there are explanations, synonyms, or examples that help explain their meaning.

Read the sentences just before and after the unfamiliar word. Often, though not always, they contain signals of explanations such as *that is*, *such*, or *in other words*. You might also find signals of examples such as *for example*, *such as*, or *for instance*. Sometimes punctuation such as dashes or commas signals an explanation, as well.

A Read the sentences from the text below. Use the highlighted signal to help you figure out what the word in italics means in the surrounding context. Look at the context before and after the word. Underline the explanation that you find.

1. They very quickly learn the way that their society expects males and females to behave and think. That is, they learn their *gender roles.*

2. Little girls are generally socialized to be *ladylike* – polite and quiet.

3. As a result, boys may grow up with a fear of being feminine and, as young men, try to keep up a *macho*, that is, very masculine, image.

4. Boys play *rough* games with their friends. They are physical and competitive in their play. (No signal)

5. For example, they may require their daughters to come home earlier at night and forbid them to go to places where they might let their sons go. Such *protectiveness* often discourages girls from being independent and exploring their environment.

B Compare answers with a classmate.

4 Answering short-answer test questions

You will often be asked to write short answers to questions about texts you read in college. It is a good idea to use words from the question in your answer, to use only relevant information from the text, and to give examples where possible.

A Read the question, text, and sample answer below. Pay special attention to the highlighted parts of the text and how they are used in the answer.

Question: *According to the text, what is the definition of socialization?*

Text: Socialization is the process of transferring values and standards of behavior to the new members of a group so that they can fit into society. There are differences in the way parents talk to their children. Parents use words about feelings and emotions more with girls than with boys, and, by age two, girls use these words more than boys do. Furthermore, mothers and fathers talk differently because of their own socialization experiences. Mothers tend to talk more politely. They may say, "Could you turn off the TV, please?" whereas fathers tend to use more direct language, "Turn off the TV." By age four, girls and boys have learned to imitate these conversational styles.

Answer: Socialization is the way that society teaches its values and culture to a new group. For example, parents talk about feelings and talk more politely to their daughters. As a result, girls learn to use this kind of language when they talk to other people.

B Read the questions and sample answers below. Highlight the information in each answer that comes from the question. Then decide if it is a good answer.

1. According to the text, how are baby boys and baby girls treated differently?
   Boys and girls wear different clothing. Boys usually wear blue, and girls usually wear pink.

2. According to the text, how are boys and girls socialized to behave differently?
   Boys are girls are socialized to behave in different ways. For example, parents talk more about emotions and talk more politely to their daughters.

C Answer each question in one or two sentences. Use information from the question and "Growing Up Male or Female" in your answer.

1. According to the text, how do peers contribute to boys' and girls' socialization?

_____

_____

2. According to the text, how do parents' expectations contribute to the way that girls behave later in life?

_____

_____

3. According to the text, why do parents find it difficult to raise their children in a gender-neutral way?

_____

_____

D Compare answers with a classmate.

1 Examining graphics ⓡ

> Remember that before reading a text, you should look at any graphs, tables (charts), or diagrams. By doing this, you can quickly get a good idea of the text's content.

Look at the table (Table 3.1). Answer true (*T*) or false (*F*) about the following statements.

F **1.** The table is about university students' achievement on standardized tests.

F **2.** The table shows that males in the study performed better than females in all areas.

T **3.** The table shows that males in the study performed better in math than females.

2 Predicting ⓡ

> Reading the title, headings, and first sentence of each paragraph first can help you predict what the reading will be about. This can help you understand better when you read the whole text.

A Read the title and the headings. Then read the following definition.

achievement *noun* something you have done successfully
Winning the science competition was a great achievement.

B Discuss the following questions with a classmate.

1. What do you think *academic achievement* means?

2. What do you think the text "Gender and Academic Achievement" will discuss?

C Read the first sentence of each paragraph of the reading. Then decide whether you think the statements are true (*T*) or false (*F*).

___ **1.** There has been a significant gap in boys' and girls' academic achievement.

___ **2.** The gender gap in achievement is increasing.

___ **3.** Male and female brains are very different.

___ **4.** Today, there is growing concern about boys' performance.

Reading 2

GENDER AND ACADEMIC ACHIEVEMENT

Schools used to offer separate courses on the basis of gender in the United States and many countries in Europe. Traditionally, typing and cooking courses were for girls; business and mechanical courses were for boys. High school teachers were not likely to encourage girls to go
5 on to college because girls were expected to get married and stay home to raise children. If a girl was going to college, teachers advised her to choose a traditionally feminine career such as teaching, nursing, or social work. Not surprisingly, in the past, boys' academic achievement was consistently higher than girls' academic achievement, especially
10 in math and science.

This picture began to change starting about the 1970s. Increasingly, schools in most countries began to offer the same courses to all students, and today both boys and girls are expected to have careers after they graduate. However, even after boys and girls began to take
15 the same courses, different expectations for boys and girls remained common. Various studies showed, for example, that from preschool through high school, girls were given less attention than boys. This gender bias may have been unintentional, but 30 years of research showed that it occurred in almost all education settings. Researchers
20 consistently found that teachers devoted more time and attention to boys than to girls. Boys were invited to participate more frequently in class and received more praise for their participation, especially in math and science classes. This may explain, in part, the lower achievement of girls in math and science.

Academic achievement of girls

25 Even though scientific studies have shown that there are some biological differences between male and female brains, these differences are too small to explain the difference in boys' and girls' achievement. As a result, researchers have looked for other reasons for this gender gap in achievement. Studies show that at
30 age nine, the majority of girls are confident, assertive, and positive about themselves. Their math and science scores are equal to boys' scores. However, when they reach high school, their self-esteem and their performances in math and science decrease. Research on the difference between girls' and boys' performances in math and science
35 suggests that it is a result of different expectations, that is, what others expect of them, and what they expect of themselves.

why - several

cause- effect

Today, however, in general, girls are doing well academically, according to the results of an international test of 15-year-olds. Historically, girls had performed somewhat better on reading and
40 writing tasks, and the gap has begun to widen in recent years. In contrast, the gap in math and science has also begun to close (see Table 3.1). Perhaps even more important, in industrialized countries all over the world, more women than men are finishing high school and are going on to a university education.

45 Scholars and educators are not certain why these changes have taken place, but there are several theories. One theory is that there are economic reasons for women's superior performance. Men can often get good jobs even without a lot of education. It is harder for women to do this. Another possible reason is the attitude among
50 boys that it is not "cool" to do well in school. Finally, some educators believe that schools now emphasize skills, such as reading and writing, and behaviors that favor girls over boys. Girls tend to mature earlier than boys and are better able to follow classroom rules, plan ahead, and to meet deadlines.

55 Consequently, in the United States and other countries, concern about academic achievement is shifting from girls to boys. Boys and young men have more social problems than girls and young women, both at school and after school. They are more likely to commit crimes and more likely to end up in prison than young women. These
60 problems increase with young men who have not completed school. It is therefore increasingly important for educators to find ways to keep boys in school and to improve their academic achievement.

Table 3.1. Mean scores of 15-year-olds by country and gender (2006)

Country	Science		Math		Reading	
	Males	Females	Males	Females	Males	Females
Australia	527	527	527	513	495	532
Belgium	511	510	524	517	482	522
Canada	536	532	534	520	511	543
Czech Republic	515	510	514	504	463	509
Denmark	500	491	518	508	480	509
Finland	562	565	554	543	521	572
Germany	519	512	513	494	475	517
Greece	468	479	462	457	432	488
Hungary	507	501	496	486	463	503
Italy	477	474	470	453	448	489
Japan	533	530	533	513	483	513
Korea	521	523	552	543	539	574
Mexico	413	406	410	401	393	427
Poland	500	496	500	491	487	528
Portugal	477	472	474	459	455	488
Switzerland	514	509	536	523	484	515
Turkey	418	430	427	421	427	471
United Kingdom	520	510	504	487	480	510
United States	489	489	479	470	NA	NA
Average Scores	501	499	503	492	473	511

Source: OECD Factbook 2010: Economic, environmental and social statistics.

1 Reading for main ideas Ⓡ

A Each of the sentences below expresses the main idea of one of the paragraphs in the reading. Match each sentence to the correct paragraph number.

5 _1_ **a.** There are several possible explanations for why girls are beginning to do better than boys in school.

1 _9_ **b.** Historically, there has been a gender bias in schools.

3 _3_ **c.** Biological difference cannot explain the gap in achievement between boys and girls, so scholars are looking for other explanations.

4 _2_ **d.** The gender gap in math and science achievement is getting smaller.

6 _6_ **e.** Today, educators are becoming more concerned about boys' academic achievement.

2 _5_ **f.** Even after boys and girls began to take the same classes, boys enjoyed advantages.

B Compare answers with a classmate.

C Write the main ideas in order.

2 Summarizing Ⓦ Ⓡ

> Sometimes you will need to write a short summary of a text, for example, if you refer to another text when you are writing an essay. To write a summary, you need to understand the main ideas in the text and then find a way to put them into just a few sentences.

A Review the ordered sentences from Step C of Reading for Main Ideas.

B Choose the best ending for a sentence that gives the two main ideas of the whole text.

The text "Gender and Academic Achievement" mainly . . .
a. describes how boys and girls do not receive the same amount of attention in school and how this results in an achievement gap.
b. describes gender-based differences in achievement and offers possible explanations for these differences.
c. discusses the many different ways that schools give messages to boys and girls about gender roles and how they respond to these messages.
d. describes the different kinds of problems that girls and boys have in school and discusses ways to resolve these problems.

C Now, use the space below to plan a summary of "Gender and Academic Achievement." Remember that your answer to the multiple-choice question in Step B (above) includes two ideas. Write one of them in the space for "Idea 1" and the other in the space for "Idea 2." Under each idea, write two sentences in your own words that provide support for it.

Idea 1 _____

_____

_____

_____

_____

Idea 2 _____

_____

_____

_____

_____

D Put all of the sentences together to make a one-paragraph summary of the reading. Begin with your sentence from Step B.

E Compare summaries with a classmate.

3 Cues for finding word meaning Ⓥ Ⓡ

Academic texts contain many unfamiliar words. Sometimes the author includes a definition for these words with signals to the definition. The word *this* is often a signal word. It tells you that there are clues to the meaning of the unfamiliar word in the context, usually in the sentence or sentences right before it.

A Reread the excerpts from the text below. Highlight the words or phrases that *this* is pointing to.

1. Various studies showed, for example, that from preschool through high school, girls were given less attention than boys. This gender **bias** may have been unintentional, but 30 years of research showed that it occurred in almost all education settings.

2. . . . these differences are too small to explain the difference in boys' and girls' achievement. As a result, researchers have looked for other reasons for this gender **gap** in achievement.

B Match each boldfaced word to the correct meaning:

1. bias
   a. harmful treatment by someone in authority
   b. special attention
   c. unfair preference for one group over another

2. gap
   a. difference between two things
   b. preference in treatment
   c. increase in an activity or action

4 Using adverbs Ⓦ Ⓡ

Sometimes you will see adverbs, such as *fortunately*, *increasingly*, and *finally* at the beginning of a sentence. Adverbs in this position can have several functions:

1. Adding detail to the information in the rest of the sentence
   Slowly, the economy is beginning to show signs of recovery.

2. Giving information about the writer's perspective
   Strangely, she had never mentioned her son.

3. Connecting two sentences
   The delivery arrived late. *Consequently*, we were unable to finish the project.

Consider the sentences from the text. Write the number of the function of the adverb (*1*, *2*, or *3*, as described above) in the blank for each sentence. You may need to look back at the text. Paragraph numbers are in parentheses.

__2__ a. Traditionally, typing and cooking courses were for girls; business and mechanical courses were for boys. (Para. 1) tradition

__2__ b. Not surprisingly, in the past, boys' academic achievement was consistently higher than girls' academic achievement. (Para. 1)

__1__ c. Increasingly, schools in most countries began to offer the same courses to all students. (Para. 2)

__1__ d. Historically, girls had performed somewhat better on reading and writing tasks, and the gap has begun to widen in recent years. (Para. 4)

__3__ e. Finally, some educators believe that schools now emphasize skills, such as reading and writing, and behaviors that favor girls over boys. (Para. 5)

3 __2__ f. Consequently, in the United States and other countries, concern about academic achievement is shifting from girls to boys. (Para. 6)

5 Applying what you have read ®

Discuss the following questions with your classmates.

1. Who generally did/does better in your school? Boys or girls?
2. Were/are girls or boys better at particular subjects?
3. Do you think the results at your school would be similar to those in Table 3.1?
4. What do you think might be the reasons for the gender gap in achievement?
5. The scores reported in Table 3.1 are from 2006. Do you think the achievement levels of boys and girls will change in the future? Why or why not?

1 Thinking about the topic ®

A Think about how men and women are portrayed in different types of mass media. Make some notes in the chart below.

Type of Media	Women	Men
Television	Shy seriously	control
Movies	Shy victm	agresive strong
Magazines	more fancy	don't care
Computer games	good body stregh clothe	strong noise

B Discuss what you have written in the chart with your classmates.

2 Increasing reading speed ®

College students often have very long reading assignments. They need to develop a fast reading style. A good goal is to read about 250 words per minute. To increase your reading speed, use the following techniques.

- Try to focus on groups of words, not on individual words.
- Try not to backtrack (go over the text again and again).
- Guess at the general meaning of words that you do not know.
- Skip over words that you do not know and that do not seem very important.
- Slow down slightly for key information, such as definitions and main ideas.
- Speed up for less important information, such as examples and details.

A Quickly read the text on the next page using these techniques.

B Calculate your reading speed.

Write your reading time _____
Number of words: 1,012 words
Divide the number of words by your time.
Write your speed: _____ words/minute

Reading 3

THE INFLUENCE OF MASS MEDIA ON GENDER ROLES

There are many agents of socialization that influence gender roles, including parents, schools, and peers. The **mass media** is another very important agent of socialization. Magazines, television, movies, advertisements, and video games all affect the way we view the roles of
5 women and men and how we think they should behave. Traditionally, they tended to define the female role in terms of the home and motherhood and the role of men in terms of work and action.

Television commercials, for example, have until recently presented women primarily as sex objects or as dutiful homemakers. Today,
10 advertisers are more careful, and they present women in a variety of professional roles, such as doctors, athletes, and artists. One study found that these changes are mainly on nighttime television, however, with daytime commercials still tending to portray women doing household chores such as cleaning and cooking. It is also still quite
15 common to see advertisements in which beautiful young women are dressed in sexy clothes in order to sell cars or other products.

Gender and body image

Socialization into gender roles affects how we behave. It also affects how we look – or want to look. The physical appearance of women in the mass media is very different from the appearance of most ordinary
20 women. In general, women in the media are taller, but they also weigh much less, which means they are very thin. Many movies use younger, thinner women as "body-doubles" for close-ups of female movie stars. All of these thin, beautiful women in the media may result in negative **body images** for ordinary women. Body image is how people perceive
25 their own bodies. One Canadian study found that 90 percent of girls and women were unhappy with their physical appearance. Most of them wanted to be thinner. An American women's magazine surveyed their readers in 2010. Over 71 percent said they were too fat.

Women are not alone in their concern about their bodies. Research
30 shows that many young men today also have a negative body image. Many of them think they are thinner and less muscular than they really are. They think they should be more muscular and athletic. However, because men are socialized not to care about their appearance as much as women do, it may be difficult for them to discuss their feelings
35 about their bodies.

mass media
communications media that reach a large audience, for example, television, newspapers, and the Internet

body image
a person's perception of his or her body's appearance

Changing stereotypes in the mass media

Stereotypes of women have also appeared on many television programs in the past. Women were usually shown as weaker and more passive than men. These kinds of roles can still be seen today, for example, in many of the *telenovelas* from Latin America. However, today's
40 television programs also offer a broader range of roles for women. They are more likely to be presented as successful, professional, and able to support themselves and their families. In movies, there are also stronger and more independent female roles than in the past. For example, the American actress Angelina Jolie has played several
45 action roles in which she is more powerful than her male co-stars. Yet, even when women are shown as successful professionals and assertive characters, the storylines often suggest that they should be sexy, as well.

Television programs also include stereotypes of men. Many
50 male characters are portrayed as capable, strong, and ready to fight to defend themselves or to protect others. Using their power and strength, they can gain the respect of other men and attract women. They rarely show their emotions. This stereotype reinforces the idea that men should always be strong and in control and that showing
55 their feelings is a sign of weakness. However, as with female characters, this picture is changing. Some television programs now include male characters who are willing to show weakness and are able to talk about their feelings.

Comics are another source of gender-role socialization. Perhaps
60 the best example is in Japanese manga, in which males are usually dominant and females are generally dependent and submissive. Some stories do include strong women characters. However, even those characters are usually looking for a man who will protect them. Western comics, too, are filled with male superheroes
65 and helpless women. Many also often include violence against women.

A relatively recent form of mass media is the computer game. These games usually include male heroes and often portray women as victims. Recently, however, there have
70 been more strong female characters in videogames, such as *Lara Croft: Tomb Raider*, *Heavenly Sword*, and *Bayonetta*. These female characters, although powerful, are also sexualized. Their images have exaggerated physical features and their clothing often barely covers their bodies.

75   Messages about gender and gender roles are all around us. Initial
socialization into gender roles occurs in the family, but these messages
are reinforced by other agents, such as schools, employers, and the
mass media. Because gender is one basis for **social inequality,** that
is, privileges and access for some groups but not for others, it is
80 especially important to understand these messages about gender
and gender roles.

Home and motherhood, care, passive
successful, profesional, and able to support theme self
sex objects or as dutiful homemakers
household chores such as cleaning and cooking
woman are dressed in sexy clothes (cars, product)
scessful, profesional and able to support
their bodie because media

1 Reading for main ideas ®

A Answer the questions.

   1. In the past, what messages did television commercials usually give about women?

   2. How does the mass media affect body image for women and men?

   3. How have portrayals of women in television changed?

   4. How are women usually portrayed in computer games?

B Check your answers with a classmate.

C Fill in the box to calculate your percentage correct on the reading comprehension questions in Step A. At 250 words per minute (wpm), a good goal is about 70 percent accuracy.

   a. wpm (from page 72) _____

   b. number correct _____

   c. percent correct (a x 100) _____

2 Reading for details ®

A Review the reading. Put a check mark (✓) if there is information in the reading about each of these topics.

	In the Past		Today	
	Men	Women	Men	Women
Television advertisements	☐	☐	☐	☐
Television programs	☐	☐	☐	☐
Movies	☐	☐	☐	☐
Comics	☐	☐	☐	☐
Computer games	☐	☐	☐	☐

B Compare charts with a classmate.

3 The passive voice Ⓦ Ⓡ

> Sentences in the passive voice are found frequently in academic writing, so it is important to be able to recognize the passive voice and understand its use.
> Writers use the passive voice when they want to do the following:
> - focus on the person or thing that the action is happening to
> - not focus on the person or persons doing the action
> - focus on the action itself

A Find five examples of the passive voice, such as the one given below, in the text and discuss with a partner why the passive voice is used.

Women were usually shown as weaker and more passive than men.

The focus is on the women, not on the television programs that show them.

B Rewrite the sentences below in the passive voice. Omit the active subjects, as in the example, if you think they are not necessary.

1. Filmmakers still typically cast men in stronger roles than women.

<u>Men are still typically cast in stronger roles than women.</u>

_____

2. Advertisements these days often show men taking care of children and cooking dinner.

_____

_____

3. Fifty years ago, TV producers cast women only in roles as mothers and homemakers.

_____

_____

4. Television directors now show women in roles that have traditionally been men's.

_____

_____

5. Advertisers still very often portray women in stereotypical gender roles.

_____

_____

6. Many movies show men as powerful and sometimes violent.

_____

_____

4 Describing people Ⓥ Ⓡ

Many different words describe personal characteristics. The text contains descriptive adjectives for men and women and their traditional or modern gender roles. Some of the adjectives below can be found in the Academic Word List. These words are listed with an asterisk (*).

assertive (5)	helpless (7)	*professional (2,5)
*capable (6)	independent (5)	submissive (7)
*dominant (7)	muscular (4)	successful (5)
dependent (7)	*passive (5)	
dutiful (7)	powerful (5,8)	

A Find the words from the list above (paragraph numbers are in parentheses) in the text and decide whether they describe someone who is strong (e.g., a leader) or someone who is weak (e.g., a follower).

Strong   Weak

_____   _____   _____

_____   _____   _____

_____   _____   _____

_____   _____

_____   _____

B Circle the correct adjective in parentheses according to the information in the reading.

1. Many modern television programs portray women as (dependent / independent).

2. In Japanese manga, the male characters are usually (dominant / submissive).

3. Most television programs have male characters who are (dutiful / capable).

4. Many of the female roles in *telenovelas* are (powerful / passive).

5. Even when roles for women are (helpless / assertive), they are often sexualized.

5 Applying what you have read Ⓡ

A Television commercials and cartoons often reflect the gender roles of society. Watch some television commercials, or look at some comics or cartoons. With a classmate, discuss the different ways in which men and women are presented.

B Find one advertisement or cartoon that you think is typical of the way men and/or women are presented. Write a short explanation of what you think is the role or image of the man and/or woman in the advertisement or comic. Use the passive voice and some of the adjectives from the previous tasks where they are appropriate. You can begin like this:

In this advertisement/comic, the man/woman is . . .

Chapter 3 Academic Vocabulary Review

The following words appear in the readings in Chapter 3. They all come from the Academic Word List, a list of words that researchers have discovered occur frequently in many different types of academic texts. For a complete list of all the Academic Word List words in this chapter and in all the readings in this book, see the Appendix on pages 213–214.

Reading 1 Growing Up Male or Female	Reading 2 Gender and Academic Achievement	Reading 3 The Influences of Mass Media on Gender Roles
traditional focus (v) furthermore intense neutral transfer (v)	academic commit consistently devote emphasize mature (v)	feature (n) initial perceive primarily reinforce sources

Complete the sentences with words from the lists.

1. The students' grades on their writing assignment depended on how much they improved between their _____ draft and their final draft.

2. Doctors _____ the importance of exercise and a healthy diet.

3. The heat at the Equator can be very _____ .

4. Until recently, the heroes in most television programs were _____ men.

5. His feelings about the election were _____ . He did not care who won.

6. Teenagers receive messages about body image from many different _____ .

7. Every day the teacher _____ some class time to a discussion of the day's news.

8. Girls usually _____ more quickly than boys, both physically and emotionally.

9. The little boy's most attractive _____ was his curly brown hair.

10. Many students of English discover that _____ language is somewhat different from the language of everyday conversation.

11. Students in the United States _____ score lower on the PISA test than do students from many other countries.

12. When parents teach their children how to behave, they are trying to _____ their norms and values to the next generation.

Developing Writing Skills

In this section you will learn about the introductory paragraph. This paragraph sets the tone for your essay and informs the reader what it will be about. You will write an introductory paragraph here. You will also use what you have learned here to complete the writing assignment at the end of this unit.

Writing an introductory paragraph

An introductory paragraph has several important elements:

- Introduction to the topic: You should have one or two sentences that tell the reader what you will be writing about.
- Main idea statement: This sentence should tell the reader the main idea of your report or essay. It should make a claim; in other words, it should say something important about the topic.
- Road map: There should be one or two sentences that tell the reader about some of the subtopics you will discuss and in what order.

You should always begin with the first element: Tell the reader what your topic is. The main idea statement may come next or it may come at the end of the paragraph.

A Read this example of an introductory paragraph about the influence of mass media on how young people learn about gender roles. As you read it, pay attention to the elements of an introductory paragraph.

Young people today get their information about gender roles from many different types of media.	• This sentence tells what the essay will be about.
They watch television and movies, they look at videos on YouTube, and they listen to music.	• This sentence tells some of the subtopics the writer will explore. This is the road map sentence.
Increasingly, however, the most important influence is online computer games.	• The last sentence makes a claim about the connection between gender roles and the media. This gives the main idea of the essay. Readers will expect to see some evidence for this claim later in the essay.

B In the sample below, label the three elements of an introductory paragraph. Some elements may include more than one sentence.

> The number of young people who have a negative body image is growing. We receive messages from many sources about what our bodies should look like – from our parents and from our peers. However, the loudest and most powerful messages come from the media. In magazines and films and on television, young people see ideal bodies: The women are tall, thin, and beautiful, and the men are tall and muscular.

C Now you will write an introductory paragraph about **gender socialization** based on information you collect from your classmates or friends. Follow the instructions below.

In this chapter you have learned about a variety of socialization agents: family, school, friends, and the mass media. All of them make important contributions to how children learn their gender roles.

Your assignment is to find out about your classmates' or friends' experiences of socialization and which influences they think were the most important. You will only write an introductory paragraph.

1. With a partner, write five questions to find out what people and institutions were the most influential. Be sure at least one of your questions asks them to rate the importance of socialization agents. One example is given below.

> When you were younger, how did you learn about gender roles and expectations from members of your family? Can you give an example?

2. Each of you should ask at least four classmates or friends to answer your questions. Take notes about their responses.

3. Discuss the responses with your partner. **Which was the most important influence across all of the responses**?

4. Now write your introductory paragraph. Be sure to include the three elements.
   a. State your topic.
   b. Give the reader some idea about the information you would discuss in the rest of the essay (which you will not actually write). This should be based on the information you collected from your classmates.
   c. Make a claim about this topic. This should be based on your answer to Question 3 – Which was the most important influence?

5. Proofread your paragraph, and make sure there are no grammar, spelling, or punctuation errors.

Chapter 4
Gender Issues Today

PREPARING TO READ

Thinking about the topic ®

A Look at these newspaper and magazine headlines. Discuss with a small group:

1. What do you think each article will be about?

> • Fathers Happier if They Do Housework
> • Husbands Closing the Gap in Housework
> • **Men Create More Housework for Women**
> • **Study Confirms Wives Do Most Chores**

2. What topic do all the articles have in common?

B Look at the family situations listed below. For each situation, discuss with your classmates who should be responsible for the following:
cooking, cleaning, taking care of children, and paying the bills.

• The husband works and the wife stays home.

• The wife works and the husband stays home.

• Both husband and wife work, but the husband earns more.

• Both husband and wife work, but the wife earns more.

Reading 1

BALANCING HOME AND WORK

Here is one family's story of balancing home and career. Anne and Martin have two children and they both work full-time.

Anne: I really have two full-time jobs. I am a pharmacist, and I love
my job. But I have another job – taking care of the kids and
5 our home. I like this job too, and I know it's important. But
when I am done with cleaning up the kitchen after dinner,
doing the laundry, and helping with homework, I get so tired
that I can't even read a book. Martin travels all the time for
his job and sometimes he doesn't get home until late in the
10 evening, so he doesn't have time to help out very much.

Martin: I work for a software company, and we all have to work really
hard to keep up with the competition. Sometimes I work 10
or 12 hours a day. I have to travel to Asia about once a month.
I want to spend more time with my children and help Anne
15 around the house, but I just can't take time off from work.
Last week I stayed home with my son when he was sick, and
my boss was very unhappy about it. I had to work late for the
next week to catch up.

Division of labor

Anne and Martin are experiencing *role conflict*. That is, it is difficult
20 for them to manage their roles at work and in their family. Role
conflict is one of the challenges that many parents face.

Balancing work and family can be a struggle for everyone, but it usually has been the woman who does most of the childcare and housework, even in homes where both parents work. However, as
25 more women have entered the workforce, this division of labor has begun to shift. Men have begun to take more of the responsibility for work in the home. A study of 20 industrialized countries from 1965–2003 revealed that men's contributions to housework (cleaning, childcare, food preparation, and shopping) had increased on average
30 from 20 to 33 percent. A study of American parents showed men's contribution to housework doubled during that period, from 15 to 30 percent, but the biggest increase was in the time that fathers spend in childcare. Fathers in the study did about 40 percent of the childcare.

Figure 4.1

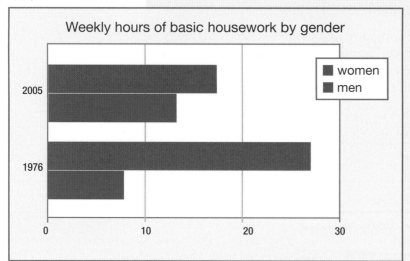

Source: U-M Institute for Social Research (ISR) Panel Study of Income Dynamics

In spite of this shift,
35 most studies of housework conclude that women (whether employed or not) still do most of the housework and childcare.
40 An Australian study, for example, found that employed wives did 69.3 hours of work around the house during a
45 two-week period whereas employed husbands did approximately 31.2 hours. A study of U.S. households showed that women spent
50 26 hours a week on housework in 1976, compared to 17 hours in 2005 (see Figure 4.1). Men's contribution to housework during the same period went from 6 hours to 13 hours. The study also showed that after marriage, women gain 7 hours of household work per week whereas their husbands work 1 hour less in the home than before
55 their marriage. Children increase housework for both of them. Three children result in 28 hours a week for mothers and 10 hours a week for fathers.

A changing role for fathers

Two careers in one household can be challenging, especially when there are children. Most mothers and fathers want to spend more time
60 with their families. A recent study of more than 1,000 working fathers in England found that 82 percent of them wanted to spend more time

on childcare. Surprisingly, the study also found that the fathers who did more housework and spent more time with their children were happier than fathers who did not help as much at home.

65 According to the author of the study, the problem is not the fathers. They want to do more. The problem is employers who have not responded to changes in family life. This can be a disadvantage for both men and women. Employers assume that a woman's commitment to her career will decrease when she has children. This can reduce
70 her chance to advance in her career. Fathers have a different problem. Employers may expect a man to have complete commitment to his career. Many employers do not offer fathers any flexibility to balance their work and home life. These attitudes and policies reinforce gender stereotypes in the workplace.

75 Families are changing and so are gender roles. Men no longer assume that they will be the sole providers for their families. Women no longer expect to take sole responsibility for their families. Children do not expect their mothers to be available all the time. In one father's words:

80 "I'd never considered the idea my wife wouldn't work. Neither had she. We wouldn't have had enough money to eat if we'd had to rely on what I was earning when our first child was born 18 years ago. And by the time I was making enough to support the family, the kids wouldn't have wanted my wife at home micromanaging their lives" (the *Guardian*,
85 Nov. 4, 2010).

The "Housework Gap"

The "housework gap" is apparent even among very well-educated couples. A study of female scientists revealed that they do nearly twice as much housework as male scientists do. When biologist Carol Greider received a telephone call to tell her that she had been awarded the 2009 Nobel Prize, she was doing laundry.

1 Reading for details ®

A Circle the correct answers to the following questions. Circle all that apply.

1. What is the point of Anne and Martin's story?
   a. You should not work full-time if you are a woman with children.
   b. It can be difficult to combine full-time work and raising a family.
   c. Women do all of the housework even if they work full-time.
   d. Men's careers prevent them from helping at home.

2. What does research tell us about the way most men and women share housework today?
   a. Men are starting to take more responsibility for work in the home.
   b. Most husbands and wives share the household chores equally.
   c. Women still do most of the housework.
   d. Men have significantly increased their participation in child care.

3. What do studies suggest about men's attitudes toward work in the home?
   a. Men want their wives to do the household chores.
   b. Men resent the extra work at home.
   c. Most men would like to spend more time on child care.
   d. Men feel happier if they help with the housework.

4. Why is it so hard to find a good life–work balance?
   a. Men want their wives to earn money and take care of the home.
   b. Employers do not offer flexibility to their employees.
   c. Women must give up their careers if they want to have children.
   d. Employers do not want to hire women.

B Compare answers with a partner.

C Explain the meaning of the following terms to your partner:

- role conflict
- division of labor
- sole provider

D How does the cartoon illustrate the *division of labor*?

2 Word families ®

> In academic texts writers use both nouns and verbs to describe behavior and attitudes. The noun and verb forms are usually very similar. There are several common suffixes that can change a verb into a noun. In some cases, however, there is no change at all. The verb and the noun are the same word. Here are some common suffixes:
>
> -tion -ment -ance/-ence

Verb	Noun
*assume	assumption
advance	advancement
balance	balance
*commit	commitment
*contribute	contribution
*reinforce	reinforcement
*rely	reliance
shift	shift

* = AWL words

Choose the correct form from the chart for the blanks in the sentences below.

1. Parents today try to find a(n) _____ between their jobs and their families.

2. Many parents do not want to _____ all of their time and energy to their careers.

3. Employers should not make a(n) _____ that women will give up their jobs for their families.

4. There has been a(n) _____ in the responsibility for child care in many homes.

5. Unfortunately, some policies have resulted in a(n) _____ of traditional gender roles.

6. Traditionally, men's _____ on their wives' work in the home allowed them to advance in their careers.

7. Some men do not _____ very much to household chores.

8. Career _____ may require employees to work long hours and do a lot of traveling.

3 Personalizing the topic ®

A Fill in this chart for your household (current or past). Check (✓) the appropriate column.

In your household, who mainly does each job?	Men/boys	Women/girls	Both equally
Shopping for food	☐	☐	☐
Preparing meals	☐	☐	☐
Washing dishes	☐	☐	☐
Vacuuming	☐	☐	☐
Cleaning bathrooms	☐	☐	☐
Taking care of the children	☐	☐	☐
Doing repairs	☐	☐	☐
Collecting the trash	☐	☐	☐
Doing laundry	☐	☐	☐
Driving/taking children to school and activities	☐	☐	☐
Helping with homework	☐	☐	☐
Paying bills	☐	☐	☐

B Compare answers with a small group and discuss:

1. Who does the most housework – males or females?
2. Are there some chores that are typically done by males? Females?
3. Are some jobs usually shared?
4. Is there any pattern to the division of labor?
5. What factors influence the division of labor?

4 Responding to a quote Ⓐ Ⓡ Ⓦ

There are many kinds of essay questions on tests. You may be asked to respond to a quote that illustrates the basic points of a topic you have studied. In order to answer effectively, follow these steps:

- Study each question carefully. Does it have more than one part? What does each part ask you to do?
- Consider how the quote is related to the material you have been studying.
- Try to use parts of the quote in your answer.
- Add your own ideas if the question asks for them.

A Reread the quote from the father in the last paragraph. Explain the ways in which it illustrates ongoing changes in gender roles. Then give your own view of whether this is a typical attitude among parents today in your country.

B Discuss the quote with a small group. Use these questions as a guide:

1. Which parts of the quote relate to traditional gender roles?
2. Which parts of the quote illustrate more modern gender roles?
3. How does this man's view compare to attitudes in your country?

C Plan your response. It will have two parts because the question asks for two things.

1. Select which parts of the quote you will use in the first part.
2. Make some notes from your discussion about how these relate to changes in gender roles.
3. Makes some notes for the second part about gender roles and attitudes in your country.

D Now write your answer to the test question.

Skimming ®

Before reading a text, remember that it is a good idea to look at any headings or graphics and to think about what kind of information they give about the text.

A Read this list of headings from the text "It's Not So Easy Being Male." With a partner, discuss what information might be in each section.

1. The Provider role

2. Emotional stereotypes of men

3. Men's health disadvantages

B Look at the table (Table 4.1) at the end of the reading. Does that affect your predictions about what the text will be about?

C Now read the following extracts with your partner, and guess which part of the text each one comes from. Write the number of the heading from Step A.

a. ___ In 2009, in the United States, the average life expectancy for men was 75.6 years whereas for women it was 80.8 years.

b. ___ Ask a man who he is, and he will tell you what he does.

c. ___ Because our culture expects a man to earn money, his salary is often connected to his self-esteem.

d. ___ Society still requires them to remain tough and competitive.

e. ___ There is some evidence that male hormones increase the chances of heart attacks.

D Scan the text to check your answers.

Reading 2

IT'S NOT SO EASY BEING MALE

The male gender role is a complex one to fulfill. It is true that males are likely to enjoy many advantages. They usually earn more than women. Also, they generally have a greater **self-esteem**, and more confidence. They are also less likely than women to experience
5 **discrimination** because of their gender. However, men do experience some disadvantages throughout their lives.

The provider role

Just as women are more often pushed toward the roles of wife and mother, men are pushed into the role of provider for their families. They have little choice – their wives, children, parents, in-laws, and
10 peers expect it. As a result, a man's identity may be strongly connected to his job. His *identity* lies in his work. Ask a man who he is, and he will tell you what he does. In studies of unemployment during the Great Depression, job loss was regarded as a greater shock to men than to women, although the loss of income affected both. It is no
15 different today – it can crush a man's self-esteem if he loses his job.

Because our culture expects a man to earn money, his salary is often connected to his self-esteem. He, as well as friends and family, may equate its size with his success. Our society encourages us to think that a man who makes a lot of money is more of a man than the
20 one who makes less.

The identification of self through work and the pressure to make money can become a problem when it pushes other concerns – such as family life – out of the picture. Many men get too caught up in their jobs and do not have enough time for their families. This can put a
25 strain on their relationships with their wives and children.

Emotional stereotypes of men

Our stereotypes of masculinity portray men as brave, strong, self-reliant, confident, and always in control. These seem like positive *traits*, but even positive stereotypes can cause problems. Some men want to be more open, expressive, and caring. In recent years, many
30 men have experienced a conflict between the stereotype and their own feelings as society urges them to express the gentle side of their personalities. At the same time, society still requires them to remain tough and competitive.

These two opposing expectations can be very stressful for men.
35 They may be unable to express feelings of depression, anger, and fear. Instead, they keep all of their feelings inside. If they do not keep their emotions under control, there may be negative consequences for

self-esteem
a person's sense of his or her worth, or value

discrimination
unfair treatment based on a specific characteristic, such as race or gender

them. Men and boys who do not conform to the expectations of their gender roles may face disrespect or even humiliation.

Men's health disadvantages

40 Men have one other major challenge in comparison to women. They do not live as long. In 2009, in the United States, the average **life expectancy** for men was 75.6 years whereas for women it was 80.8 years. This five-year difference is typical of industrialized countries. In other parts of the world, the difference is even larger (see Table 4.1).
45 In spite of the significant health risks of childbirth for women, this has remained consistent all over the world for as long as modern records have been kept.

Many researchers have tried to find out why this difference in life expectancy is so persistent. Some have suggested that men's lives are 50 more stressful because of the pressure to provide for their families. Other suggestions are that men tend to participate in more dangerous activities. They are more competitive, and they take more risks. As a result, they are more likely to have accidents or experience violence. In addition, men are more likely to have unhealthy habits, such as 55 smoking and drinking, which may shorten their lives.

However, recent research suggests that the biggest reason for the difference in longevity is out of their control because it is biological. There is some evidence that male hormones increase the chances of heart attacks and female hormones provide some protection against 60 heart disease. In general, women's hearts maintain their power to pump blood longer than men's hearts. Again, some scientists believe that hormones explain the difference. Whatever the reason for it, this gap between men's and women's life expectancies is decreasing in most industrialized countries. Unfortunately, the gap is increasing in many 65 developing nations, where life expectancy is already much lower than in industrialized nations.

Men have many advantages in life, but they also face a number of challenges, including conflicting expectations and biological disadvantages. As gender roles become more equal, it is possible that 70 these challenges will decrease.

life expectancy
average expected length of life

Table 4.1. Life expectancy at birth by region and sex

	Women			Men		
	1990–1995	2000–2005	2005–2010	1990–1995	2000–2005	2005–2010
Africa						
Northern Africa	68	72	73	64	68	69
Southern Africa	64	51	52	59	49	51
Eastern, Middle and Western Africa	54	55	57	50	52	54
Asia						
Eastern Asia	74	76	77	69	71	72
South-Eastern Asia	66	70	72	62	66	67
Southern Asia	59	65	67	57	62	64
Central Asia	68	70	70	61	61	62
Western Asia	72	75	76	67	71	72
Latin America and the Caribbean						
Caribbean	75	76	77	69	71	72
Central America	73	76	77	67	70	71
South America	72	75	76	66	69	70
Oceania	68	71	73	64	67	68
More developed regions						
Eastern Europe	75	76	77	66	68	69
Western Europe	80	82	83	74	76	78
Other more developed regions	80	83	83	74	77	78

Source: The World's Women

1 Pronoun reference Ⓦ Ⓡ

When reading, it is important to keep track of how pronouns – for example, *he*, *she*, *it*, *they*, *this*, *that*, *these*, *those* – may be used to refer to people, things, or ideas in a previous or subsequent sentence.

Reread the excerpts from the text below. Highlight the referent of the pronoun shown in *italics*.

1. Because our culture expects a man to earn money, his salary is often connected to his self-esteem. He, as well as friends and family, may equate *its* size with his success.

2. The identification of self through work and the pressure to make money can become a problem when it pushes other concerns – such as family life – out of the picture. Many men get too caught up in their jobs and do not have enough time for their families. *This* can put a strain on their relationships with their wives and children.

3. In other parts of the world, the difference is even larger. In spite of the significant health risks of childbirth for women, *this* has remained consistent all over the world for as long as modern records have been kept.

4. Again, some scientists believe that hormones explain the difference. Whatever the reason for *it*, this gap between men's and women's life expectancies is decreasing in most industrialized countries.

2 Answering definition questions on a test Ⓐ Ⓡ Ⓦ

In college there are different kinds of test questions. One common type of question asks you to write a definition of an important term. You can predict what some of those terms will be by looking for words in boldface in your textbook. As you read, you should try to predict which definitions might be on the test.
A good way to write a definition is to refer to a larger category and then give some specific information about it. The specific information should say why it is different from other things in that category.

Example: dictionary

- A dictionary is a book that gives definitions of words.
- A dictionary is a book with definitions of words.
  In these definitions of dictionary, the sentences refer to a larger category – books – and then describe what kind of book it is.

A Review the text and find the words in bold and italic.

B In the task below, fill in the first blank in each item with the correct boldfaced or italicized term from the text. In the second blank in each item, provide some specific information to complete the definition.

1. _____ is a person's belief _____ .

2. _____ is treatment _____ .

3. A person's _____ is the quality _____ .

4. _____ is a characteristic _____ .

5. _____ is the average length of time _____ .

C Turn back to the readings in Unit 1. Write three more definitions of terms that you think might be on a test.

3 Describing personality and emotion Ⓥ

The words in the list below are all related to personality, feelings, and emotional responses. Write the letter of the correct definition. (The paragraph where the words appear is given in parentheses.) Academic Word List words have an asterisk (*).

1. ___ *self-reliant (adj) (5)   **a.** showing what you think or feel

2. ___ confident (adj) (5)   **b.** a feeling of deep unhappiness and hopelessness

3. ___ expressive (adj) (5)   **c.** a situation in which ideas, feelings, or opinions are in

4. ___ gentle (adj) (5)   opposition to each other

5. ___ *conflict (n) (5)   **d.** feeling or state of shame and embarrassment

6. ___ competitive (adj) (5)   **e.** not needing help from other people

7. ___ humiliation (n) (6)   **f.** sure of your abilities and value

8. ___ *depression (n) (6)   **g.** kind and soft

                          h. wanting to be more successful than others

4 Going beyond the text Ⓦ Ⓡ

In the chapter you have been reading a lot about gender stereotypes – what they have been in the past and how they are changing. There are also other kinds of stereotypes, for example, about people from different parts of the world.

A Are there stereotypes about people from your country? What are they? Do you think these are correct and fair?

B Write down a few notes for yourself about your responses to the questions in Step A. Be sure to include some descriptive adjectives.

C Share what you have written with a small group of your classmates.

• If your classmates are from the same country, ask them to add their ideas to your description.

• If they are from a different country, answer any questions they have about your description.

D Choose one of the stereotypes you have discussed. Write up a short explanation of your stereotype. Your explanation should have two parts. The first part should state what the stereotype is. The second part should express your opinion of the stereotype.

First part:

One stereotype of ＿＿＿＿＿＿ is that they are ＿＿＿＿＿＿＿＿＿

＿＿＿＿＿＿＿＿＿＿＿＿＿＿＿＿＿＿＿＿＿＿＿＿＿＿＿

＿＿＿＿＿＿＿＿＿＿＿＿＿＿＿＿＿＿＿＿＿＿＿＿＿＿＿

＿＿＿＿＿＿＿＿＿＿＿＿＿＿＿＿＿＿＿＿＿＿＿＿＿＿＿

＿＿＿＿＿＿＿＿＿＿＿＿＿＿＿＿＿＿＿＿＿＿＿＿＿＿＿

For example, ＿＿＿＿＿＿＿＿＿＿＿＿＿＿＿＿＿＿＿＿＿＿

＿＿＿＿＿＿＿＿＿＿＿＿＿＿＿＿＿＿＿＿＿＿＿＿＿＿＿

＿＿＿＿＿＿＿＿＿＿＿＿＿＿＿＿＿＿＿＿＿＿＿＿＿＿＿

＿＿＿＿＿＿＿＿＿＿＿＿＿＿＿＿＿＿＿＿＿＿＿＿＿＿＿

Second part:

In some ways this stereotype is true because ＿＿＿＿＿＿＿＿

＿＿＿＿＿＿＿＿＿＿＿＿＿＿＿＿＿＿＿＿＿＿＿＿＿＿＿

＿＿＿＿＿＿＿＿＿＿＿＿＿＿＿＿＿＿＿＿＿＿＿＿＿＿＿

＿＿＿＿＿＿＿＿＿＿＿＿＿＿＿＿＿＿＿＿＿＿＿＿＿＿＿

OR

However, the stereotype is not really accurate because ＿＿＿＿

＿＿＿＿＿＿＿＿＿＿＿＿＿＿＿＿＿＿＿＿＿＿＿＿＿＿＿

＿＿＿＿＿＿＿＿＿＿＿＿＿＿＿＿＿＿＿＿＿＿＿＿＿＿＿

＿＿＿＿＿＿＿＿＿＿＿＿＿＿＿＿＿＿＿＿＿＿＿＿＿＿＿

1 Previewing art ®

Before reading, it is a good idea to look at any art that accompanies the text. It can help you think about what information will be in the text.

A Look at the cartoons in the text and read the caption. Discuss the questions below with a classmate.

    1. What does the first cartoon illustrate?

    2. The second cartoon is based on a common expression "A penny for your thoughts," which means, "What are you thinking about?"

       • What do you think the "gender gap" means in the cartoon?

       • What do you think the caption means?

B What does the second cartoon illustrate?

2 Predicting ®

A Skim the title and the headings in the reading.

B Read the definitions below

disparity

a lack of equality and similarity, especially in a way that is not fair

workforce

the group of people who work in a company, industry, or country

C Write one sentence describing what you think the text will be about.

Reading 3

GENDER EQUALITY AT WORK

In the past, women did not have the right to vote, to go to school, to borrow money, to own property, or to work in certain occupations. Women who worked usually made far less money than men. Underlying these inequalities has been a prejudice against women
5 that is based on **sexism**. Over the years, women have fought for their rights, and now gender equality is protected by a number of laws and rulings in many countries of the world.

sexism
discrimination based on gender

One of the areas where women have fought for equality is in the workplace. They have made great progress toward this goal. However,
10 women remain unequal to men economically. It is still typical for women to hold lower-status, lower-paying jobs than men. In many traditionally female occupations – such as nursing, teaching, and secretarial work – women work in positions that are subordinate to positions usually held by men.

15 Thus, nurses are often subordinate to male doctors, teachers to male principals, and secretaries to male executives. Many people still like it this way. One survey asked Americans if they preferred a man or a woman in jobs that are traditionally male or female. Many respondents said they would prefer a woman as an elementary
20 schoolteacher and a man as a police officer and airline pilot.

Many countries have passed laws to prohibit gender discrimination in employment. The United States passed a law against gender discrimination in 1963. This means, for example, that a company may not advertise a job for men only. It also means that employers must pay
25 men and women the same wage for jobs that require the same skill,

effort, and responsibility. Similar laws followed in the 1970s and 1980s in Europe and in other parts of the world. Since then, women have made significant gains in the workplace. More women are working (see Figure 4.2), and their pay is higher than ever before.

The continuing gender disparity

30 The disparity in wages between men and women in employment remains in spite of these laws. Some researchers believe that one reason is women's commitment to the family. One study found:

> The majority of women . . . want to pursue serious careers while participating actively in the rearing of children . . . most of them are
35 > willing to trade some career growth and compensation for freedom from the constant pressure to work long hours and weekends.

However, this is probably not the most important reason. A report by the World Economic Forum found that a major factor is the male-dominated culture in many workplaces. All over the world,
40 women enter the workforce in jobs that are lower paying and have lower statuses than men's, regardless of their level of education. The Organization for Economic Cooperation and Development reports that in industrialized
45 countries, men earned an average of 17.6 percent more than women in 2006. The biggest disparity was in South Korea, where the wages for men
50 are almost 40 percent higher than for women. Belgium had the smallest difference at 9.3 percent. Even when women hold the same jobs as men and
55 have equal skills, training, and responsibility, they tend to earn less. In the United States, women's wages are 77 percent of men's wages for the same job.

'Three-fourths of a penny for your thoughts..'

Women as a growing part of the workforce

60 In spite of their lower pay, women's overall participation in employment is increasing rapidly. Women now hold over 50 percent of all management and professional jobs in the United States. This is an increase of 26 percent since 1980. A study of 20 industrialized countries shows that women are in the majority in financial and professional
65 services. In China, more than 40 percent of private businesses are owned

by women. Women currently dominate 13 out of the 15 jobs that are predicted to have the highest growth in the coming decades. However, it is important to note that these are not the jobs with the highest pay.

Why is this happening? It may not simply be a result of laws or 70 a decrease in discrimination. It is possible that the modern, **post-industrial economy** favors women. Industrial jobs favored men's size and strength. In contrast, post-industrial jobs require people with communication and social skills. These are attributes generally associated with women. Many of these new jobs emphasize creativity 75 and working as a team, rather than competition and taking risks. Finally, today's jobs often require a high level of education. Since today more women than men are getting a college education, women are often more attractive to employers.

Gender equality in employment is the law in most Western 80 countries now. However, in reality, the disparity in pay remains. Women have made great progress in closing the gap in recent years, but full equality still remains a goal for the future.

post-industrial economy when the importance of manufacturing decreases and the importance of services, information, and research increases

Figure 4.2. Percentage of women in the workforce in 2009

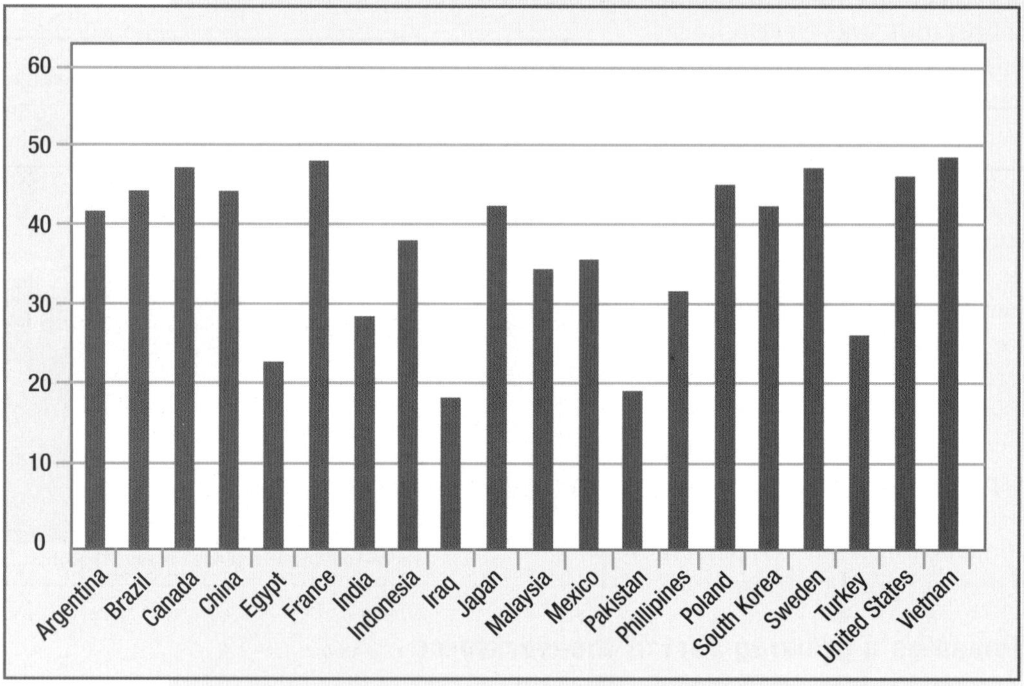

Source: United Nations Dept of Economic and Social Affairs

1 Reading for main ideas ®

A Which of the following states the main idea of the text? Put a check (✓) by your choice.

___ **1.** Women remain unequal to men in employment although most countries have laws that require equal pay.

___ **2.** Men and women earn equal pay in most countries, but there are still more men than women in the workplace.

___ **3.** Women have made advances in the workforce, but they have not yet reached full equality.

B Discuss your choice with your classmates. Explain why you think your choice is the best one.

2 Supporting main ideas Ⓦ Ⓡ

> Identifying evidence for the main idea in a text can help deepen your understanding. Charts are a useful way to keep track of supporting ideas. They can also help you plan your own writing.

A Review your choice from the previous task. Notice that the main idea has two parts.

B Reread the text, including Figure 4.2, to find evidence for each of the two parts. Make notes in the chart below. Include the paragraph number where you found the evidence. One example is provided for you.

Evidence for women's advances	Evidence of continuing inequality
In many countries laws require gender equality in the workplace. (Par. 1)	Women usually have lower-status, lower-paying jobs. (Par. 2)

C Use the chart to answer the following test question.

> According to a United Nations report, women have made great progress in their fight for equality. However, there is not yet complete equality for men and women in the workplace. What evidence is there to support this statement?

3 Guessing meaning from context Ⓥ Ⓡ

> Often you can figure out the meaning of new words from the surrounding context. There may be examples that can help you figure out the meaning.

A Look back at the text and review the context where these words or phrases appear. Look for examples that may explain their meaning. The paragraph number is in parentheses. Academic Word List words have an asterisk (*) before them.

- lower *status (2)
- *subordinate to (2)
- *prohibit (4)
- *attributes (8)

B Write the word or phrase in the blank before the correct meaning.

_____ stop
_____ less respected
_____ characteristics
_____ lower than

C What clues in the reading helped you figure out the meaning?

4 Collocations Ⓥ Ⓡ Ⓦ

> Remember that it is a good idea to be aware of collocations when you read.

A Scan the text and find the verbs that co-occur with these nouns. In some cases they may appear with more than one verb. The paragraph in which each noun appears is in parentheses.

_____ money (1)

_____ money (1)

_____ progress (2)

_____ a job (2)

_____ laws (4)

_____ wages (4)

_____ gains (4)

_____ a career (5)

_____ an education (8)

B Write three sentences about the gender gap in wages. Use one of the collocations in each sentence.

5 Thinking critically Ⓡ Ⓥ

With a small group of classmates, discuss the following questions. Try to use some of the vocabulary you have learned from the text.

1. Do you think men are better for some jobs and women are better for others? If so, which ones?

2. Do you think there is still gender discrimination in the workplace in your country?

3. Have you ever experienced gender discrimination at work?

4. Can you think of any examples of women who have broken through gender discrimination and have become very successful?

Chapter 4 Academic Vocabulary Review

The following words appear in the readings in Chapter 4. They all come from the Academic Word List, a list of words that researchers have discovered occur frequently in many different types of academic texts. For a complete list of all the Academic Word List words in this chapter and in all the readings in this book, see the Appendix on pages 213–214.

Reading 1 Balancing Home and Work	Reading 2 It's Not So Easy Being Male	Reading 3 Gender Equality at Work
apparent approximately contribution labor (n) period sole (adj)	complex (adj) discrimination equate maintain persistent stressful	compensation cooperation goal occupations pursue underlying

Complete the sentences with words from the lists.

1. The math problem was very _____ ; it had many steps. The student found it difficult.

2. Her _____ in life has always been to become a doctor.

3. The flight from London to Sydney lasts _____ 21 hours.

4. It is important to _____ a healthy weight so you avoid health problems.

5. He always enjoyed math and science, so he decided to _____ a degree in engineering.

6. Women have often experienced _____ in the workplace. They may earn less than men who do the same work.

7. When you look for a new job, you should consider many factors, but for most people, _____ is probably the first. Everyone has to pay bills.

8. Some _____ , such as that of a secretary and a teacher, are often associated with women.

9. Money is not the _____ factor in choosing a job. Working conditions are also important.

10. It is a mistake to _____ physical maturity with emotional maturity.

11. When the new workers made mistakes, it became _____ that they needed more training.

12. Girls quickly understand the _____ message of many advertisements – "thinner is better."

Practicing Academic Writing

In this unit you have learned about gender roles from a variety of perspectives. Based on everything you have read and discussed in class, write an essay about the following topic:

Gender Preferences

Using your own experience as well as the information in Unit 2, answer the question "Is it better to be a man or a woman?" You will write a "Yes, but . . . " essay. This means you will acknowledge some points that are the opposite of your own point of view and then show that your point of view still makes more sense.

Making a list

Before you start writing, you need to gather some ideas to write about. A list is a simple way to get started. You may not use all of the ideas in your list. You may add to your list as you begin writing. The process of writing is not always a straight line. Sometimes you may want to come back to the Preparing to Write section and reconsider your ideas.

A Review the readings in this chapter. Keep in mind the questions in the assignment: Is it better to be a man or a woman? Make notes on any important points in the readings that you would like to use in your essay.

B Make a list of important points on both sides of the issue. These points may be from the readings or from your own experience. One example is provided for you.

Better/easier to be a woman	Better/easier to be a man
Less pressure to earn money	Less discrimination

C Exchange lists with a classmate and discuss the points on your lists.

D Based on your list and discussion, decide which point of view you will take.

E Write a sentence that states the main claim you want to make. This sentence will have to contrast the two points of view. This statement tells the reader it will be a "Yes, but . . . " essay. For example:

> • Although men have many advantages in life, I think it is easier to be a woman.
> • Men have many advantages in life; however, their lives are still more difficult than women's lives.

F Review the points in your chart. Choose two or three points on each side that you would like to discuss in your essay.

G Decide if one of the points is more important than the other(s).

NOW WRITE

A Review the assignment on introductory paragraphs from Chapter 3. The sentence you wrote in Step D above will be your *main idea sentence*. It makes the central claim of your essay. Now complete the rest of the introductory paragraph. Be sure to include all three elements.

- Statement of your topic
- Your claim about the topic (your main idea sentence)
- Road map for the rest of your essay

B Write a body paragraph that includes at least two points that take the perspective that is **the opposite of yours**. Review the writing assignment in Chapter 1 on body paragraphs. As you write this paragraph and the one in C, below, remember:

- Every body paragraph should have a topic sentence.
- Your evidence should be in order of importance. Either begin or end with your most important or persuasive support.

C Write a body paragraph that states **your** point of view and your two or three reasons. Use information from the readings and examples from your own experience or knowledge.

Revising

It is important to be able to review your own writing, but it is sometimes easier to begin with work written by others. Looking at someone else's writing can help you see your own writing with "new eyes."

A Review the body paragraph below. It expresses the author's point of view. Highlight

- the topic sentence and
- the strongest or most persuasive piece of evidence.

When both the husband and wife have a career, it can be difficult to get all the housework done. It is true that men have increased their contribution to work in the home in the last 20 years; however, many of them still expect their wives to do most of the work. This is true even if the husband and wife work the same number of hours. Wives work on average twice as many hours doing housework and childcare as their husbands. In fact, marriage increases their work considerably. Research shows that married women spend almost twice the number of hours doing housework as single women.

B Now reread your own essay. Check that

- it has an introductory paragraph with a general statement and a main idea sentence that shows two different points of view;
- it has one body paragraph that states the opposite point of view with two or three pieces of supporting evidence;
- it has a second body paragraph that states your point of view with two or three pieces of supporting evidence; and
- each body paragraph has a topic sentence.

C If any elements are missing or need to be changed, make a note of the revisions you will make.

D Consider the topic sentences in your two body paragraphs.

- Do they make it clear which point of view is yours?
- Does the topic sentence in your second body paragraph acknowledge the opposite point of view but make your point of view very clear? In other words, does it make a "Yes, but . . . " argument? Here is an example of a sentence that expresses "Yes, but . . .":

All of these facts make a man's life seem very challenging (YES); however, the advantages that men have are greater than the disadvantages (BUT).

E Reread the body paragraph in Step A. Which is the "Yes, but . . . " sentence in the paragraph? Underline it.

F Review the task on Showing Contrast on pages 59–60. Can you use one of the linking words to revise the topic sentence in your second body paragraph? This topic sentence should be a "Yes, but . . . " sentence that shows the contrast between the point of view in the first body paragraph and your own point of view in the second body paragraph.

G Exchange essays with a partner. Review his or her paper.

- Does it have an introductory paragraph with general statement and main idea sentence that shows two different points of view? Underline the main idea sentence.
- Does it have a paragraph that states the opposite point of view with three pieces of evidence that support it? Number them.
- Does it have a paragraph that states the author's point of view with three pieces of evidence that support it? Number them.
- Does each body paragraph have a topic sentence? Underline them.
- Is the topic sentence in the second body paragraph a "Yes, but . . . " sentence?
- Does the author use information from the readings? If not, can you suggest any information that the author should include?
- Does the author include facts or examples from his or her own experience or knowledge?

H Revise your essay.

- Review your partner's suggestions.
- Review your own notes for revision.
- Make necessary changes.

I Edit your essay.

Read through your essay now for possible spelling mistakes, punctuation errors, subject-verb agreement errors, incorrect use of past tense, and article usage. Make corrections whenever you find errors.

Unit 3
Media and Society

In this unit you will look at the media, including newspapers, television, and the Internet. In Chapter 5 you will consider how and why we use media. You will explore who and what gets reported, as well as how far the media should go in reporting the news. In Chapter 6 you will read about recent changes in the media, in particular, the impact of computers and the Internet. You will examine ways in which these developments have changed how we get the news, how we interact, and even how we think and learn.

Contents

In Unit 3, you will read and write about the following topics.

Chapter 5 Mass Media Today	Chapter 6 Impact of the Media on Our Lives
Reading 1 The Role of Mass Media **Reading 2** What Is Newsworthy? **Reading 3** Privacy and the Media	**Reading 1** The Impact of the Internet on the Mass Media **Reading 2** Social Media **Reading 3** Learning and Thinking with New Media

Skills

In Unit 3, you will practice the following skills.

Ⓡ **Reading Skills**	Ⓦ **Writing Skills**
Personalizing the topic Reading for details Skimming Thinking about the topic Applying what you have read Reading boxed texts Predicting Scanning Increasing reading speed Reading for main ideas Previewing art and graphics	Linking ideas in a text Summarizing Road map sentences Going beyond the text Paraphrasing
Ⓥ **Vocabulary Skills**	Ⓐ **Academic Success Skills**
Words related to the topic The Academic Word List Compound words and phrases Collocations Prefixes and suffixes Guessing meaning from context	Highlighting Answering true/false questions Answering multiple-choice questions Preparing for an essay test

Learning Outcomes

Write an essay on media use based on a survey

Previewing the Unit

Before reading a unit (or chapter) of a textbook, it is a good idea to preview the contents page and think about the topics that will be covered. This will give you an overview of how the unit is organized and what it is going to be about.

Read the contents page for Unit 3 on page 110 and do the following activities.

Chapter 5: Mass Media Today

A With a partner, make a list of different kinds of mass media.

_____   _____
_____   _____
_____   _____

B In the last unit you learned about the effect of mass media on gender roles. With your partner, make a list of other aspects of our lives that are affected by mass media.

_____
_____
_____
_____
_____

Chapter 6: Impact of the Media on Our Lives

A Find out the meaning of the following words used in this chapter.

- blog
- social media
- tweet
- wiki

B With a group of classmates, discuss the ways in which these terms might be related to mass media.

Chapter 5
Mass Media Today

1 Personalizing the topic ®

Thinking about your own personal connections to a topic before you read will help you absorb new information on that topic.

A Think about your own use of mass media. Complete the chart below.

Medium	Which medium do you use for news? 1 = most often used 5 = least often used	Which medium do you use for entertainment? 1 = most often used 5 = least often used	About how many hours per week do you spend on each?
TV			
Radio			
Newspapers			
Magazines			
Internet			

B Compare charts with your classmates.

C With a group of classmates, answer the following questions.

1. If your answers are similar to your classmates', why do you think this is? If they are different, why do you think this is?

2. Do you think your parents would fill the chart out differently? Explain.

3. If someone asked you to fill out the chart 15 years from now, how do you think your answers would differ?

2 Words related to the topic Ⓥ

Work with a partner and describe each type of television program.

- drama
- reality show
- comedy
- documentary
- cartoon

Reading 1

THE ROLE OF MASS MEDIA

The term *mass media* refers to the forms of communication (*media*) that reach a large public audience (the *mass* of the population). Mass media include newspapers, magazines, film, television, radio, and more recently, the Internet. Mass media communication is often rapid
5 because the media report an important event as quickly as possible after or even as it happens. It is also transient; that is, the focus on one event doesn't last very long. The expression "there is nothing as old as yesterday's news" illustrates these two aspects of mass media.

Functions of the media

Most of us use some form of the media every day, but we may not
10 think about the functions or purposes the media serve in our society. One important function is to *inform*. We get most of the news about what is happening in the world and in our communities through the mass media. Sometimes this news has important consequences for the
15 public. For example, the media may inform the public about dangers such as air or water pollution in a community or a harmful product or drug. The media can also provide
20 other kinds of warnings. For example, the media can warn of the danger of an approaching hurricane or tornado. These warnings alert people to take the necessary precautions.
25 Without such warnings, there could be a greater loss of life and property.

Many people listen to music and watch movies online.

Another important function of the media is *entertainment*. On television, in particular, there are many different kinds of programs that provide entertainment, such as dramas, comedies, cartoons,
30 and reality shows. Different kinds of programs appeal to different viewers, depending on age, gender, and interests. Some programs also have an educational function beyond their entertainment value. These include documentaries on a wide range of topics such as animal behavior, geography, history, or art. There are also a variety
35 of instructional programs such as cooking, home repair, or investing. Some children's programs are also educational, teaching children to count or to recognize words or introducing them to different societies and cultures.

A further function of the mass media is *socialization*. The media
40 provide one way for a society to transmit cultural values about what is appropriate behavior to its members. People may be socialized

into behaving in certain ways in response to a personal problem, for example, because they have frequently seen others on the news or in television dramas behaving that way in similar circumstances. In
45 general, the media have an important role in shaping our beliefs.

Finally, for some people the media offer *companionship*. Television personalities may be seen as "friends" by their viewers, particularly if those viewers are socially isolated, elderly or sick, and in need of companionship.

Recent developments in mass media

50 The media change with developments in technology. The most important recent change in mass media is the growth of the Internet. Today, more and more people get their news, information, and even education from the Internet. All of the traditional forms of mass media – newspapers, magazines, film, television, and radio – are
55 now available on the Internet. Recent studies show that people are increasingly turning to the Internet instead of these traditional media. A 2009 survey showed that almost 70 percent of adult Internet users in the United States now watch videos online. They can also get news, information, and entertainment on a computer or on a mobile device
60 such as a cell phone or portable music player.

Another important aspect of the media on the Internet is the widespread participation of ordinary people. In traditional media, journalists and broadcasters decide on the content, and people

watch, read, or listen. Information moves in one
65 direction. Today, anyone with a computer and a connection to the Internet can be the author of media content. Ordinary people can upload a video, post their views on a blog, or publish a news story online. Information moves in
70 many different directions at once. This change also means these new authors can decide what is important. They can write about news events and politics, but they can also write about their children, their pet turtle, or where to buy the
75 best cup of coffee. Blogs have become extremely popular. In 2011, there were more than 150 million blogs on the Internet. It is all part of the face of the *new media*.

More and more people get their news online.

The range of functions and sources of the media in society are
80 many and varied, and their influence on our lives is considerable. The media influence how we spend our time and our money, what we get to see and hear about, and the way we understand those events. They help to shape our beliefs, our opinions, and our behaviors.

1 Reading for details Ⓡ

A According to the text, what are two important aspects of *mass media* communication?

Rapid

transient

B What are four functions of mass media?

To inform

Entretaiment

Socialization

offer comporonship

C Name two ways in which the Internet has changed mass media.

Growth of the enternet

widespred partapation of ordinary people.

2 Linking ideas in a text Ⓦ Ⓡ

Sometimes large sections of a text across several paragraphs will provide a series of examples. This kind of organization of a text is often signaled with these kinds of phrases:

- *There are many kinds of / examples of / functions of . . . One X is . . . another is . . .*
- *The functions of / causes of . . . are many. They include . . .*

Linking expressions may be used to show that another idea is being added to the list. Some common words used to link ideas in a text include: *another*, *further*, *also*, *and*, *secondly*, *finally*, and *in addition to*.
If it is clear that a text is presenting a series of ideas, a linking expression may not be necessary to signal that this is the next idea in the list. Understanding these organizational features will help you to follow the meaning of the text.

A Underline the part of the text in Paragraph 1 that signals to the reader that a list of different types of media will follow.

B Paragraphs 2 through 5 list and explain the main functions, or purposes, of mass media. Complete the chart with the functions and the linking expressions used to introduce them.

Par.	Functions of mass media	Linking phrases and words
2	new about happening in world	one funtion
3	diferent programs	important fution
4	to transmit	A further fuction
5	TV	Finally

3 Highlighting Ⓐ Ⓡ

Highlighting is a useful strategy for quickly marking important information in a text when you are studying for a test or doing research. However, simply highlighting information will not necessarily help you recall it. You will need to review that information and perhaps make notes from it.

A Read the paragraph below. It presents facts about media use in the United States. Underline the media mentioned and highlight the relevant facts and figures.

Mass media is an important part of life in the United States. People are exposed to the media daily in the form of print, sounds, and pictures. Newspapers have been an important source of the news for a long time. However, newspaper circulation is declining in the United States. In 2009 it dropped by more than 10 percent. In contrast, television continues to be a very popular source of news and entertainment. The average American household has 2.5 television sets; 31 percent of households have four or more televisions. The amount of time that Americans spend in front of their television sets varies with age, gender, and education, but on average it amounts to more than 35 hours per week.

B Record the highlighted information in note form in the space below.

Form of Media	Facts
1)	
2)	

C Now do the same thing – underline, highlight, and take notes – on the "Recent developments in mass media" section (Paragraphs 6 and 7) of the text.

4 The Academic Word List Ⓥ

A Review the description of the Academic Word List (AWL) on page 104. The words below come from the AWL.

B Match the words from the text in the left-hand column to their meanings in the right-hand column. Write the letters on the lines.

_h_	**1.** illustrates	**a.**	alone, separate
_g_	**2.** focus	**b.**	conditions, situation
_e_	**3.** approaching	**c.**	in many places
_i_	**4.** range	**d.**	made available in print
_f_	**5.** participation	**e.**	coming near
_b_	**6.** circumstances	**f.**	act of taking part in an activity
_a_	**7.** isolated	**g.**	center of attention
_j_	**8.** device	**h.**	shows by example
_c_	**9.** widespread	**i.**	set of similar things
_d_	**10.** published	**j.**	machine

C Complete the sentences with the 10 AWL words from Step B.

1. We heard a loud sound from the _____ train.

2. The new school has a special _____ on mathematics and science.

3. The newspaper _____ a series of stories about the terrible fire that killed more than 100 people.

4. There was _____ concern all over the city about the safety of drinking water after a factory released dangerous chemicals into the river.

5. The company put a small _____ in each of its offices to record all conversations.

6. The hotel offers a wide _____ of services to its guests, including an exercise room, a swimming pool, computers, and fax machines.

7. An increase in the number of car accidents caused by teenagers _____ the importance of driver's education in schools.

8. The small village in the mountains is very _____ . The closest town is 50 miles away.

9. The soldiers must live in very difficult _____ . They sleep on the floor, and they often do not have enough food.

10. The teachers in this school believe that parents' _____ in their children's education is very important.

1 Skimming Ⓡ

> Remember that skimming involves reading parts of a text such as subheadings, opening sentences of paragraphs, or words in italics or bold.

A Skim the text looking at the words in italics. After you have finished, write down the words you recall.

B Repeat the exercise. This time look quickly for information to explain the terms.

2 Thinking about the topic Ⓡ

> If something is *newsworthy*, it has value, or *worth*, as news, and the public will probably be interested in hearing or reading about it in the media.

A Read the information below about news events. Rate them to show if you think they would be newsworthy to an American living in San Francisco.

1 Very newsworthy   2 Somewhat newsworthy   3 Not newsworthy

___ **a.** A fire destroys a church in Greece.

___ **b.** The U.S. president gets sick and cancels meetings for two days.

___ **c.** An elderly San Francisco couple celebrates their 50th wedding anniversary with family and friends.

___ **d.** There is a shooting at a shopping center outside of San Francisco.

___ **e.** A traffic accident stops traffic for three hours in Berkeley, a city across the bay from San Francisco.

___ **f.** An earthquake occurs in Mongolia.

___ **g.** An earthquake occurs in Los Angeles.

___ **h.** Two people are murdered in Buenos Aires.

B Discuss your choices with a small group. Why are some stories newsworthy and others not? Make a list of factors that make a story newsworthy.

Reading 2

WHAT IS NEWSWORTHY?

Of all that is happening in the world, very few events or people appear in the news. Why? What determines if an event or a person is *newsworthy?* There are a number of factors that influence why and how events are reported.

5   *Negative events* are more likely to be reported than positive ones. News of current events is often bad news. Such news includes natural disasters, such as earthquakes and floods, or accidents that involve damage, injury, or death. Consider how much of the news is about conflict between people, political parties, or nations. Once an event 10 is identified as newsworthy, the negative aspects of the event may be highlighted through the use of strong negative language in the headline or story.

   The time of an event is also important. The media are most likely to report something that has just happened. The language of the story 15 and of the headline tends to stress the immediacy of recent events. Headlines in the news most frequently use the present tense, rather than the past tense, for example "Bomb explodes in train station."

This makes the event seem closer in time. News on cable television and the Internet report 24 hours a 20 day, but newspapers and many major television and radio stations operate on a daily news cycle. Shorter events that fit into this time span are more likely to be reported than those that last longer. Therefore, a murder is more newsworthy than a long police 25 investigation of the murder; the verdict at the end of a trial is more likely to be reported than a whole trial.

   Another important factor that determines what is newsworthy is *fame.* Famous people are more newsworthy than ordinary people. The public is 30 especially interested in celebrities, such as movie stars, singers, and athletes. Sometimes an event can become news just because a celebrity is involved. If the same story were about an ordinary person, it would simply be ignored. For example, there was constant media attention when movie 35 stars Angelina Jolie and Brad Pitt had a baby or when Mel Gibson got divorced or made a controversial remark.

   Geographic proximity, or closeness, is also a key factor. The closer the place, the more newsworthy the event is. A major catastrophe from the other side of the world will be in the news. In contrast, a minor 40 crime or accident may be reported in the place where it happens but not one hundred miles away. The issue of proximity can also apply to cultural associations. In the English-language media, a story from an

English-speaking nation is likely to be considered more newsworthy than a similar story from a non-English speaking nation. When floods
45 in northeastern Australia in late 2010 and early 2011 killed more than 40 people and left many others homeless, it was reported at length in English-language media around the world. When flooding and the resulting mudslides killed almost 800 people in Brazil, the media coverage was much less extensive.

50 In general, too, *unexpected* or unusual events are more newsworthy than the ordinary and routine: a crocodile that swallows a cell phone (see boxed text), twins who are born in different years, or a man who marries a dog. Sometimes,
55 however, the media will focus on a story of ordinary people. Often, this kind of story is reported in colorful and emotional language. These are often called *human interest* stories. Some stories tell about ordinary people who
60 become heroes. For example, a customer in a supermarket finds out that one of the employees is very sick and needs a new kidney. The customer offers one of his kidneys even though he does not know her very well. Other human interest stories are sad. For example, a hardworking
65 immigrant is robbed and loses all of his money. He cannot care for his two young children. Readers respond to the emotional side of sad stories. They want to help people who are in trouble. Many human interest stories inspire the people who read or hear them. This makes them newsworthy.

70 Often news reports are a combination of breaking news – events that have just happened – stories that satisfy our curiosity about important or famous people, and stories that touch us on a more emotional level.

Crocodile Swallows Cell Phone!

A visitor at a Ukrainian aquarium told workers that a crocodile had swallowed her phone. At first, the employees did not believe it when the woman told them what happened. "But then the phone started ringing and the sound was coming from inside our Gena's stomach and we understood she wasn't lying," said an employee.

Gena, the 14-year-old crocodile that swallowed the phone, appears depressed and in pain. Gena swallowed the Nokia phone after the visitor dropped it in the water. She had stretched out her arm, trying to take a photo of the crocodile opening its mouth, when the phone slipped.

1 Applying what you have read Ⓡ

A Work with a partner. Reread the text quickly. Find and list all of the factors for newsworthiness mentioned in the text.

B Read the following news headlines. With your partner, discuss which factors from your list make each story newsworthy.

1
THE WORLD
Explosion Injures 2 at Local Factory

2
The Herald ✦
$40 Million Drug Arrest in Paris

3
THE REVIEW
Hurricane Hits Mexican Coast

4
NATIONAL TRIBUNE
Elsie Is 110 Today!

5
The Boston Times
10,000 Homeless After Chinese Quake

6
The Daily Paper
Movie Star Arrested for Drunk Driving

7
Daily News ✦
Hottest Winter Day on Record

C Read the front page of a local English-language newspaper. Decide why each news item was included.

→ 2 Reading boxed texts Ⓡ

Reread the boxed text, "Crocodile Swallows Cell Phone," and answer the questions below.

1. Do any of the factors for newsworthiness apply to the story in the boxed text? Which ones?

2. Review the reasons for the inclusion of a boxed text in academic texts after the reading "How We Learn to Behave" on page 22. Why do you think "Crocodile Swallows Cell Phone" was included in this reading?

1. Huricane Hits mexican coast, Movie star Arrested for drunk driving

2. Is an interesting example, give a definition and also ask you to apply ideas to your own life.

3 Compound words and phrases Ⓥ Ⓡ

Sometimes two words combine to make a single new word. The new word is called a *compound word.* In other cases, two words do not combine, but they appear with each other so frequently that they become *fixed phrases.* When you are reading, you can often guess the meaning of compound words and fixed phrases if you know the meaning of the two words that form them. When you are writing, however, it is often difficult to guess whether two words should be a compound word or a fixed phrase.

A Find the words or phrases below in the text and decide if they are compound words or fixed phrases. Write *CW* or *FP* in the blank in front of each item.

_CW_ cell + phone
_FP_ current + event
_CW_ earth + quake
_FP_ hard + working
_CW_ head + line
_CW_ high + light
_FP_ movie + star

_____ mud + slide
_FP_ natural + disaster
_CW_ news + paper
_CW_ news + worthy
_FP_ political + party
_CW_ super + market
_____ time + span

B Write the correct items from Step A next to the definitions below.

1. place to buy food and other products _supermarket_

2. famous actor _moviestar_

3. violent movement under earth _earthquake_

4. always doing a lot of work _hardworkink_

5. period of time _timespan_

6. very interesting, worth writing about _highlight_

7. stress, emphasize _mudslide_

8. title of a news story _headline_

9. catastrophe caused by forces of nature _natural disaster_

10. organization of people with similar political views _political party_

11. important recent occurrence or issue _currentevent_

12. mass of wet dirt and rock moving down a mountain _news worthy_

13. telephone you can use almost anywhere _cell phone_

14. printed pages that report important events _newpaper_

→ 4 Summarizing Ⓦ Ⓡ

> Remember that summarizing is an essential study skill. Writing a good summary is a way of showing that you have understood what the text is about and what the most important points are.

Use seven of the words listed below to complete the summary of the text.

athlete	determine	immediacy	proximity
constant	heroes	inspire	recent
cycle	ignore	involve	

Many factors _determine_ if a story is newsworthy. First, negative events, such as disasters, are considered more newsworthy than positive ones. Second, _recent_ events as well as events that fit into the 24-hour news _immediacy_ are likely to be reported. Events about celebrities are more newsworthy than those that _involve_ ordinary people. _proximity_ is another important factor. People care more about events that happen near them than those that occur far away. Finally, unusual events often appear in news stories. These include truly strange events but also stories about ordinary people who become _heroes_ – stories that _inspire_ the people who read them.

1 Predicting ®

Work with a partner. Look at the photographs below.

1. Who are these people? What do you already know about them?

2. Why do you think they might be mentioned in a text about privacy and the media?

2 Thinking about the topic ®

A Work in a group. Imagine that you work at a newspaper. You have information about or photographs of the following news items:

- a politician who went on a vacation with a woman who was not his wife
- a person threatening to commit suicide by jumping off a building
- the location and size of a military unit on a secret assignment
- a movie star hitting a news reporter in the street
- a confidential message sent by an ambassador to the president
- a famous athlete drinking heavily at a popular bar
- the arrest of a famous young singer for stealing a pair of jeans from a store
- a report about how many people died in a military attack

B Discuss and decide which of these stories or photographs, if any, you will publish in your newspaper. What factors did you consider in making your decisions?

Reading 3

PRIVACY AND THE MEDIA

Media professionals often face difficult decisions about whether to publish a story, photograph, or video. Often, there are ethical issues that they need to consider. Would publication be an invasion of privacy; that is, does it contain something that should remain private? 5 Would publication be a threat to national security? Journalists must decide what responsibility they have to society and if that responsibility would be fulfilled by publishing the story.

Privacy and celebrities

An interesting question related to the media and privacy is whether the public has the right to know about the private lives of people who are 10 public figures. In 1998 the story of the relationship between President Bill Clinton and Monica Lewinsky was in the news for many months. The media published very personal details of the relationship, and the scandal almost forced the president to resign. A basic question for the media is whether a politician's personal life is relevant to his or her job 15 performance. One point of view is that if a person is not honest with his or her spouse, that person will not be honest with the country's citizens. Another view is that a person's private life does not predict his or her public performance, and everyone has a right to privacy.

Paparazzi often follow celebrities.

Other famous people, including movie 20 stars, athletes, and royalty are also closely followed by the media. They often wear disguises in public to avoid media attention. The media go to great lengths to find out about celebrities. Some journalists dig through 25 garbage cans to find little bits of information on their private lives. Some press photographers try to take photographs of them in their most private moments to sell to the world's media. Photographers often use long powerful lenses 30 so that they can take photos from a distance and spy into people's homes, for example. These photographers are called *paparazzi*.

Paparazzi have been around for decades, but their business has grown in recent years because there are now more magazines that 35 focus on the lives of famous people. With digital cameras, photos and videos can be sent quickly to publishers around the world. Paparazzi can make a lot of money, and this means that some of them are becoming even more aggressive in their efforts to get a "good" photo. Some paparazzi have been accused of deliberately starting fights 40 with movie stars in order to take pictures of them in embarrassing situations.

All of this attention is sometimes more than just a nuisance. In 1997, when Princess Diana died in a car accident in Paris, her car was being chased by paparazzi. This started a big public debate about the behavior of paparazzi and privacy and the media. In spite of this tragedy, however, the public appetite for stories about celebrities continues, and new technology is creating new opportunities for the journalists who write about them. For example, starting in 2005, several reporters at a British newspaper illegally accessed the private voice mail accounts of Prince William and Prince Harry of England. They used what they heard to write several embarrassing stories about the princes' social activities. When this was discovered, two reporters lost their jobs and served prison sentences.

Privacy and politics

The lives of celebrities are not the only important issues that involve privacy and the media. Some issues concern international relations and national security. The media sometimes publish confidential documents and stories about politically sensitive topics. In 1971, government documents about the Vietnam War were leaked to the *New York Times*. These documents, called the Pentagon Papers, gave details about political and military activities that had been government secrets. Journalists at the *New York Times* decided that the public's right to know this information was more important than the protection of government secrets. The story had an enormous influence on the public, turning opinion against the war.

A more recent example involves WikiLeaks, a Web site that publishes videos, stories, and classified documents that many governments do not want the public to see. In 2010, it published videos of a bombing raid on Baghdad, Iraq, in which many civilians died, as well as thousands of documents about civilian deaths in the war in Afghanistan. WikiLeaks also published messages between government officials. The officials expected these communications to remain private when they wrote them. In some cases, the publications led to embarrassment, and as a result, many government officials said they could no longer write candid reports. In other cases, however, the consequences were even more significant. The publication of these private communications contributed to protests and political unrest in 2011.

Journalists and others in mass media must constantly balance the interests of the public with the confidentiality of personal and government information. The right choice is often not clear, and it is rarely easy to make.

Magazine stories about celebrities are popular.

1 Answering true/false questions Ⓐ Ⓡ

True/false questions are sometimes given in tests to check your understanding of a reading passage. Read this list of strategies for answering them.

- Answer every question. You always have a 50/50 chance of being right.
- Pay special attention to statements with negatives in them. These are often tricky to answer. Remember that a negative statement that is correct is true.
- Pay attention to words like *always*, *only*, *never*, and *all*. Statements that represent extreme positions are usually false. On the other hand, more tentative statements are more likely to be true.
- Read all parts of a statement carefully. Some parts may be true, but if any part of it is false, then the whole statement is false.
- In any series of true/false questions, there are usually about the same number of true statements as false ones.

Decide if the following statements are true or false according to the information in this text. Write *T* or *F* next to each statement.

____ **1.** President Bill Clinton was forced to resign as a result of a scandal.

____ **2.** Some journalists search through garbage to find information about celebrities.

____ **3.** Digital technology has made the job of paparazzi easier.

____ **4.** In 1977, journalists illegally accessed the private voice mail of Princess Diana.

____ **5.** As a result of the release of the Pentagon Papers, all Americans began to oppose the Vietnam War.

____ **6.** WikiLeaks published information about secret activity in Iran.

____ **7.** Publication of secret documents on WikiLeaks embarrassed many officials.

____ **8.** Journalists believe that the public's right to know is always more important than a person's right to privacy.

2 Collocations Ⓥ Ⓡ

A Scan the text to find and underline the fixed noun phrases listed in Step B, below. Use the context to try to figure out their meaning.

B The left-hand column contains fixed noun phrases. The right-hand column contains examples of what these fixed phrases refer to. Write the letter of the correct example.

___ **1.** invasion of privacy

___ **2.** (threat to) national security

___ **3.** public figure

___ **4.** job performance

___ **5.** social activity

___ **6.** international relations

___ **7.** classified document

___ **8.** government official

___ **9.** political unrest

a. people march in the street calling for change in their government

b. a party

c. someone who checks passports at a national border

d. paparazzi try to take pictures at a private event

e. a bomb explodes at the president's house

f. an employee does an excellent job on a project

g. a television star

h. communication between Russia and the United States

i. a report on a secret government project

3 Road map sentences Ⓦ Ⓡ

> Academic texts often contain guiding sentences that give you some idea of the material that will follow. These are sometimes called *road map sentences.* You will usually find these sentences in the opening paragraph and then in first sentences of each subsection of a reading.

A Review the opening paragraph of the text. The first and last sentences tell the main idea of the reading. The other sentences, highlighted below, help readers by providing a road map for the rest of the reading; in other words, they point to other parts of the reading.

Media professionals often face difficult decisions about whether to publish a story, photograph, or video. Often, there are ethical issues that they need to consider. Would publication be an invasion of privacy; that is, does it contain something that should remain private? Would publication be a threat to national security? Journalists must decide what responsibility they have to society and if that responsibility would be fulfilled by publishing the story.

B With a classmate, discuss how the highlighted sentences function as a road map. In other words, what other parts of the reading do these sentences point to?

C Many of the readings in this book have sections with subheadings. These sections also usually contain road map sentences. Review the rest of the reading, paying attention to the two subheadings. Find a road map sentence in each of the sections that points to what the rest of the section will be about.

D Compare answers with a classmate.

Chapter 5 Academic Vocabulary Review

The following words appear in the readings in Chapter 5. They all come from the Academic Word List, a list of words that researchers have discovered occur frequently in many different types of academic texts. For a complete list of all the Academic Word List words in this chapter and in all the readings in this book, see the Appendix on pages 213–214.

Reading 1 The Role of Mass Media	Reading 2 What Is Newsworthy?	Reading 3 Privacy and the Media
aspect function (n) invest role survey (n) transmit	constant controversial cycle (n) injury investigation issue (n)	debate (n) enormous ethical illegally military relevant

Complete the sentences with words from the lists.

1. Thousands of people enter the country _____ every year. This is against the law.

2. I cannot sleep in my apartment because of the _____ noise.

3. There was a story on the news about a(n) _____ into drug use by athletes.

4. Many young people join the _____ to serve their countries during times of war.

5. There has been _____ growth in the popularity of social media.

6. Mass media play an important _____ in shaping public opinion.

7. The decision to go to war is always _____ . Many people disagree about it.

8. Citizens use blogs to present their views on _____ such as crime and politics.

9. A recent _____ of people between the ages of 18 and 25 showed that many of them get their news and entertainment on mobile devices.

10. One unique _____ of Internet media is its interactivity.

11. People _____ in Internet companies because they are often profitable.

12. There has been considerable _____ about the impact of the Internet on our society. Some people think it is good, but other people are more negative.

Developing Writing Skills

Sometimes you will use your own ideas to provide support for your claims. In academic writing, however, you will have to find supporting evidence from other written sources. In this section, you will use information from your readings in your writing. When you do this, it is important to put the ideas in those sources into *your own words*. This is called paraphrasing. This is an important skill that you will use constantly in your academic writing. You will practice the skill here and in the assignment at the end of this unit.

PARAPHRASING

Writing a good paraphrase is challenging. A paraphrase should be about the same length as the original material. You need to express the main ideas of the author, so you cannot make big changes. However, you cannot use the author's words. Following these steps can help you to write an appropriate paraphrase.
Read the source material carefully.

1. Make a few notes on a separate card or piece of paper. Do NOT write full sentences. Instead, just write important words, phrases, and ideas.

2. Put away the source material and be sure you have not memorized it.

3. Think about which important words you might need to use from the original text. You can use some of these words, but you should also try to use some new words.

4. However, remember that paraphrasing is not just finding synonyms. It is saying the ideas in a new and original way.

5. Remember to say where you found the original information.

6. After you write your paraphrase, compare it to the original.

   • Did you keep the basic meaning the same?

   • Have you expressed the meaning in a new and original way?

A Read the following paragraph and then study the sample paraphrases. With a classmate, decide which is the better paraphrase and explain why.

Reading 1

BLOGGING, THE NEW JOURNALISM

Original

There are many new ways to exchange news and information. The traditional media, such as newspapers and television, no longer have complete control over the news. Ordinary people now have access to the same technology as traditional journalists. They can publish their own views and even their own news stories. They don't need a job at a newspaper or television station. One of the most common forms of this new type of journalism is the blog. There are blogs about everything. As of 2006, there were more than 50 million blogs on the Internet. One important advantage of blogs is that they are fast. Stories often appear on blogs before they appear in newspapers or on the radio. For instance, during national disasters and periods of political unrest, bloggers can often report stories before traditional reporters reach the scene.

Paraphrases

1) "Blogging, the New Journalism" says that the traditional media don't control the news anymore. There are new ways to get information. Ordinary people can publish their own ideas and their own news without a job at a newspaper or television station by using new technology. Blogs are one new form of journalism. There were more than 50 million blogs on the Internet in 2006. Blogs report the news very quickly. They often publish the news before traditional media, for example, during national disasters and periods of political unrest. Bloggers often arrive and report the news before traditional journalists.

2) Blogs are the newest form of journalism. According to "Blogging, the New Journalism," there are millions of blogs. The author states that bloggers have become an important source of news, especially in situations such as national disasters and political unrest, where events move quickly. Bloggers often report on these events more rapidly than traditional journalists. This is possible because of advances in technology. Today, ordinary people, not just professional journalists, have access to this technology.

B Read the paragraph below. Follow the steps for writing a paraphrase on page 132.

How paparazzi work

Paparazzi say everyone complains about them. Yet many people still want to see their photographs, so they can be very valuable. Several factors determine the value of a paparazzi's photograph. The most important is the subject of the photograph. How famous is the celebrity? Second, what is the star doing? The price is higher if the star is doing something that would create a scandal, for example, dancing at a wild party. The quality of the photograph is also important. If the image is fuzzy, it may be difficult to identify the person in the picture. Such images will not bring a high price. Finally, is the photograph exclusive, or do lots of other paparazzi have similar images to sell? Paparazzi can sell exclusive photographs at a high price.

Chapter 6
Impact of the Media on Our Lives

1 Scanning ®

> *Scanning* is looking quickly through a text to find a specific word or piece of information, such as a name, date, or definition. When you scan, you do not read every word. Your eyes pass over the text, stopping only when you find the word or information you are looking for. You may need to do this when preparing for a test or a writing assignment.

Scan the paragraph below to find the answers to the following questions.

1. How did the Internet begin?

2. Who owns it today?

The Internet started when an office in the United States Defense Department began a computer communication network in 1969. The goal was to connect universities and government research centers through a national network of computers that would allow researchers to share information and resources. The final result of this project is a technology that has changed the nature of communication. The Internet is not owned or controlled by any person, company, or country.

2 Increasing reading speed ®

> When you are studying, it is important to be able to read quickly. You do not have time to read everything slowly and carefully.

A Review the speed-reading techniques in Chapter 3, page 72.

B Practice the speed-reading techniques as you read "The Impact of the Internet on Mass Media." Time yourself (or your teacher will time you). Try to read the text in four minutes. Then tell a partner two or three main ideas you understood from the text.

Reading 1

THE IMPACT OF THE INTERNET ON MASS MEDIA

A generation ago, if you were reading about mass media, there would be no mention of the Internet. Today, the Internet is so integrated into our lives and the media that it is hard to imagine a world without it.

The original purpose of the Internet had nothing to do with mass
5   media, and it was not intended for ordinary people. It was developed as part of a plan for military defense. Soon, however, it became clear that the Internet could do many other things. In the beginning, not very many people could use it because computers were expensive and connections to the Internet were slow. However, as computers became
10 cheaper and connections became faster, the Internet began to change the face of the media.

The Internet delivers traditional media

The Internet is able to deliver everything that traditional mass media delivers, but it provides more of it and provides it more quickly. This is possible because of two important developments in digital technology:
15 the browser and the search engine. Both of these are so familiar now that we may forget their importance. A browser, such as Explorer or Mozilla Firefox, allows users to navigate, or move around, the Internet through links. A search engine, such as Google, allows users to find Web sites about specific topics. Without these tools, all the information
20 on the Internet would be inaccessible to most people.

Figure 6.1. Uses of the Internet

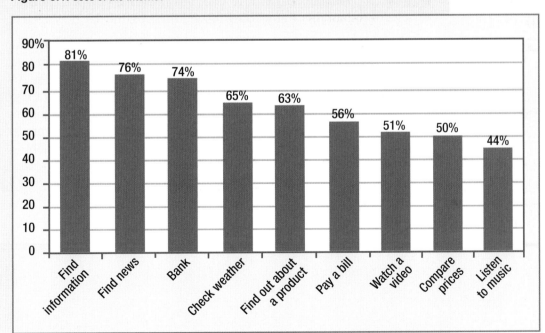

Source: OfComm Communications Market Report

On the Internet, users can search for specific kinds of information or entertainment. Anyone can find large amounts of news and information instantly. What is perhaps the most significant development is user control. Users no longer have to depend on what a newspaper or television station decides is newsworthy. Similarly, they are no longer limited to the entertainment that is on the radio or television at a particular time. Users can access programs on demand. They can also find entertainment that is not available on traditional media, such as interactive games. They can play by themselves or against other users who may be far away. In short, users can choose the news and entertainment that they want whenever and wherever they want it.

Why the Internet is different from other kinds of media

The Internet provides access and control. It is also able to deliver information that was never available from traditional mass media sources. For example, many people now depend on the Internet for health information. They also use it for shopping. Before they buy anything, they can find out about products and services on the Internet. For example, users can compare the prices of a camera from two different stores. They can read the opinions of people who have already bought the camera. They can find out about services, too, such as the location of a restaurant on a map, when it is open, what is on the menu, and what other diners think about the food there. In comparison, traditional media resources provide us with very limited information. The telephone directory usually just provides the name, address, and telephone number of a business. Newspapers publish reviews of restaurants, but we have to read them on the day they appear.

Not only has the amount of information increased but so have the sources of information. One reason is that anyone can post content on the Internet: restaurant and product reviews, political opinions, or funny videos. Many users have created their own blogs. Most of these blogs are interactive. The author posts messages with information, news, and opinions, and then readers can leave their comments in response. Many traditional media, such as newspapers and magazines, now include blogs in their online versions, but many blogs are written by people who are not professional journalists.

This two-way flow of information has another important consequence. It means that people and organizations can collaborate in the creation of new knowledge. Probably the most familiar example of this is the wiki. A wiki is a Web site that allows people to work together to create and continuously update Web pages about a particular topic. The most famous wiki is Wikipedia. Wikipedia is an encyclopedia that is created by users. Wikipedia is not the only wiki, however. There are wikis for travel, for shopping, for news, politics, music, and hundreds of other topics.

Although the Internet has brought many advances, the speed and accessibility of the medium also has drawbacks. There is so much information that it is sometimes difficult for users to sort through it and figure out which information is the most important. In addition, because anyone can post to the Internet, there is less control over the accuracy and quality of the information. It may not always be reliable, so users must be more cautious consumers of the news and information they find on the Internet.

The Digital Divide

The Internet has been a powerful force in the media, bringing massive amounts of information to the public and allowing people all over the world to share news and information. However, it is not available to everyone. The term *digital divide* refers to unequal access to digital information. Most, but not all, people in the developed world can access the Internet. However, many people in the developing world and an important minority of people in the developed world cannot afford it. They are limited to the news, information, and entertainment that is available from traditional media sources.

1 Reading for main ideas ®

A Quickly reread Paragraphs 1 through 8. Write a few words or phrases to record the main idea of each paragraph.

Paragraph 1: _The internet is so integreted into our lives and the media (Today)_

Paragraph 2: _The internet can do many other things (However)_

Paragraph 3: _(is able to)_

Paragraph 4: _Anyone can find_

Paragraph 5: _It is also able to_

Paragraph 6: _Many traditional media_

Paragraph 7: _There are_

Paragraph 8: _Altought the internet_

B Look at Figure 6.1. With a classmate, compare the uses listed there to your responses to Question 1 in "Personalizing the Topic" at the beginning of Chapter 5 (page 112).

2 Prefixes and suffixes Ⓥ ®

Many English words contain smaller units called prefixes and suffixes. *Prefixes* come at the beginning of a word, and *suffixes* come at the end of a word. There are many more suffixes than prefixes in English. If you understand the meaning of these smaller units, it will be easier for you to understand many new vocabulary words.

The example of the word *access* shows how each unit adds to the meaning of a word. *Access* is both a noun and a verb.

- access (*n*) the ability or opportunity to use something
- access (*v*) to have the opportunity to use a resource
- accessible (*adj*) If something is *accessible*, you can *access* it.
  Pattern: If something is *Xible/Xable*, you can X it.
- inaccessible (*adj*) If something is *inaccessible*, you cannot *access* it.
  Pattern: *In/unX* means not X.
- accessibility (*n*) the quality or state of being *accessible*.
  Pattern: *Xity* is the quality or state of being X.

eR → noun person

Additional Suffixes and Their Meanings			
Suffix	**Meaning**	**Example**	**Part of speech**
-er/or	X*er* is someone or something that/who does X	writer	noun
-ive	Something that is X*ive* is concerned with/characterized by X	active	adjective
-cy	X*cy* is the state of being X	democracy	noun
-ous	X*ous* means full of X	dangerous	adjective
-ful	X*ful* means full of X	forceful	adjective

A Look at the words in the chart below. Fill the blanks with words from the reading that contain suffixes.

Noun	Verb	Adjective
expense	*expensive*	_____
_____	browse	*browser*
familiarity	*familiar*	_____
availability		_____
	interact	_____
_____		accurate
	rely	_____
caution		_____
power	*powerfull*	_____
_____	consume	
mass	*massive*	_____
_____		minor

browser
explorer
expensive
deliver

B Fill each blank with the correct word from the chart. Use the correct form of the word.

1. Information on the Internet is not always _____ or _____ so you should not believe everything you read there.

2. A _____ amount of information is _____ on the Internet; in fact, sometimes there is too much information.

3. Most Internet users are _____ with _____ such as Internet Explorer and Mozilla Firefox.

4. Computers have become more _____ and less _____ in the past 10 years.

5. You should use _____ when you _____ with other people over the Internet. They may not be telling you the truth about themselves.

3 Going beyond the text Ⓦ Ⓡ

The purpose of some writing assignments is to see how well you have learned the material in your textbook or lectures. Other assignments ask you to pursue topics in your textbook further and to extend your understanding. You should be prepared to analyze new but related material.

A Review the boxed text, "The Digital Divide" and study the figure below. Then discuss the questions with your classmates. Make some notes about your discussion.

Figure 6.2. Internet use per 100 people

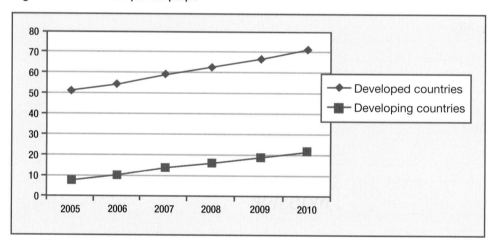

Source: International Telecommunication Union

1. What does the graph illustrate?

2. What do you think are some reasons for the facts that the graph illustrates?

3. What do you think might be some consequences of the facts that the graph illustrates?

B Make an outline for the answer to the essay question below. Use the notes from your discussion.

Many scholars believe that the *digital divide* will continue through much of the 21st century. Explain what you think will be consequences for developed and developing countries if the digital divide continues.

   I. Definition of the *digital divide*

_____

  II. Consequences for developed countries

_____

_____

 III. Consequences for developing countries

_____

_____

C Write a short paragraph based on **one** of the three sections of your outline.

1 Skimming ®

A Skim the text quickly for one minute. Read the subheadings and the first sentence in each paragraph.

B Match each question on the top to an answer on the bottom.

____ **1** "What are social media?"

____ **2** "How have social media affected interpersonal communication?"

____ **3** "How have social media affected social movements?"

     a. "provides accessible and efficient way to communicate with other members"

     b. "interactive online forms of communication."

     c. "People have friends online instead of face-to-face. Interaction can be anonymous."

2 Previewing art and graphics ®

> Looking at the graphs and photographs in a text and reading the captions is a good way to get an idea of the content.

A Look at the photographs and graph in the text, "Social Media." With a classmate, discuss what you think the text will be about.

B Write a sentence to describe what you think the text will be about.

Reading 2

SOCIAL MEDIA

What are social media?

The most important development in the recent history of mass media is undoubtedly the explosive growth of *social media*. Social media are forms of online interactive communication in which users participate in the creation of content. In 2011, social media sites like Facebook,
5 Twitter, YouTube, and FourSquare attracted millions of users. They have several common features.

- They use Internet-based technology.
- They are interactive.
- They are accessible at little or no cost to anyone with a computer
10 and an Internet connection.
- They deliver information quickly.

Social media have spread quickly and are now pervasive. A survey in 2010 revealed that people throughout the world spend over 110 billion minutes a year on social media sites. The survey also showed
15 that in the preceding year, the number of visitors to these sites went up by 24 percent, and the amount of time that an average visitor spent on them went up by 66 percent. In 2012, Facebook was the most popular, with over 845 million users (see Figure 6.3). Half of them visited the site at least once a day. Facebook even has its own currency so users
20 can buy and sell things within the site. In 2010, Twitter had almost 200 million users who sent 65 million messages, or tweets, every day. In a period of five years, YouTube went from eight million views per day to two billion. When the site first began in 2005, most of the material consisted of short, homemade videos. In 2010, in contrast, YouTube
25 had broadcast a formal interview with President Barack Obama and the Indian Premier League cricket matches.

How have social media affected interpersonal interaction?

Social media have taken over the functions of some traditional media, for example, to inform the public, but most of all, social media have changed how people interact with one another. Today, many people
30 have a large community of friends on the Internet. They may not have met some of these people face-to-face, but they share interests and experiences with them online. Most Facebook users have about 120 online friends, but some have a lot more. In 2010, Lady Gaga passed President Obama's record. She had 10 million friends.

35   Some people worry that social media users spend too much time in cyberspace, and they will become isolated from real life and real people. However, a recent survey of American Internet users suggests the opposite. The survey found that Internet users were more likely to join community, social, and political groups, and social media use was
40 an important part of their participation in those groups.

    Another concern is that the Internet and *social networking* sites like Facebook make it possible to interact anonymously. This encourages some users to say whatever they want, even if it is hurtful. There have been several shocking cases of *cyberbullying*, in which some users
45 have harassed another user anonymously. Cyberbullying includes sending hostile messages, spreading rumors, and publishing personal information or embarrassing photographs. Some victims have been so upset they have had to leave their school, workplace, or have moved to another city. A few have committed suicide as a result.

How have social media affected social movements?

50 Social media have also played an important role in *social movements*. Social movements are a form of collective behavior to promote or prevent social or political change. Some social movements are *revolutionary*, such as when the Communists came to power in China (1949) or Cuba (1959). Others, such as the civil rights movement in
55 the United States, are considered *reform* movements. Finally, the aim of *resistance* movements is to prevent change or stop outside influence. In some Muslim countries, for example, some social movements have tried to minimize Western influence.

Figure 6.3. Number of Facebook users by year (in millions)

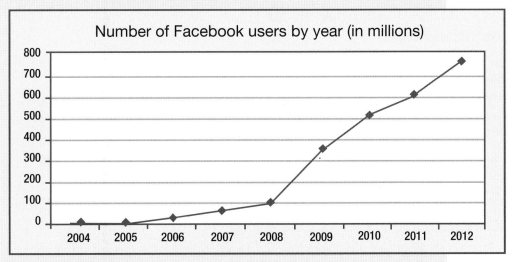

Number of Facebook users by year (in millions)

Source: Facebook.com

Social media have provided these movements with an accessible
60 and efficient way to communicate with other members of the
movement and publicize their efforts outside of the movement.
Communication occurs much faster in social media that in traditional
media. Twitter makes it easy to pick up and resend short messages.
Tweets go out as text messages and over the Internet, so people can
65 receive them on almost any digital device.

President Barack Obama used social media extensively in his 2008
presidential campaign, but the impact of social media on politics is
not limited to the United States.

Recently, social media have also played an important role in
70 political movements in North Africa and the Middle East. The 2011
political unrest spread through the use of YouTube and Facebook.
Protesters sent messages by text and on Twitter. One Egyptian named
his daughter "Facebook" several weeks after the protests. A new
leader in Tunisia sent out a tweet that said they had "the most rapid
75 revolution in history because we are connected."

1 Reading for main ideas Ⓡ

A Answer the question.

Which of the following best states the main idea of this text?
a. Political and social activists have used social media effectively.
b. Social media have significantly increased the frequency of online relationships.
c. Social media have fundamentally changed how society communicates.
d. There has been enormous growth in many forms of social media.

B Find which parts of the text are summarized by the remaining three statements.

C Compare answers with a partner.

2 The Academic Word List Ⓥ Ⓡ

A Scan the text to find the words from the Academic Word List in the left-hand column. Draw a line between the words in the left-hand column and their meanings in the right-hand column. Use the context of the word in the text to help you decide.

1. site (n)   a. show
2. feature (n)   b. money
3. survey (n)   c. place, location
4. reveal (v)   d. make smaller
5. preceding (adj)   e. characteristic
6. currency (n)   f. encourage, support
7. promote (v)   g. study
8. minimize (v)   h. previous, past

B With a classmate, answer the questions below.

1. Think of a Web site on the Internet that you visit often. What are your favorite **features** on that **site**?
2. What do you think were the most important events of the **preceding** year?
3. What is the official **currency** in your country?
4. What would a **survey** of the sleep habits of your classmates **reveal**?
5. What is the best way to **promote** healthy eating habits in children?
6. How can we **minimize** the amount of food that we waste every day?

3 Collocations Ⓥ Ⓦ

> There are many common collocations of verbs and prepositions in English. Make a note of new collocations as you learn them. The more you are aware of collocations, the easier reading becomes.

A The following verbs in the text collocate with prepositions. Write the preposition that collocates with each verb. Sometimes there is a noun between the verb and the preposition.

Verbs	Noun	Preposition
1. participate		in
2. spend	time/money	on
3. consist		of
4. interact		with
5. share	something	with
6. isolated		from
7. provide	someone	with
8. be limited		to

B Fill in the verb-plus-preposition collocations in the sentences below.

1. The small village _____of_____ twenty houses, a school, and a post office.
2. She _____with_____ her friends online at least once a week.
3. The town is _____from_____ the other towns in the valley by a large river that has only one bridge across it.
4. She _____in_____ three different sports: basketball, tennis, and swimming.
5. News coverage is often _____ events of the previous day.
6. The hotel _____provide_____ them _____ lunch and a snack for their trip.
7. He _____share_____ photographs of the class party _____with_____ his friends on Facebook.
8. They _____spend_____ all afternoon and the whole night _____on_____ their science project.

4 Personalizing the topic Ⓡ

With a partner or small group of classmates, discuss the question below.

The reading "Social Media" claims that the emergence of social media has resulted in a variety of important changes. Consider how social media have changed your life or the life of someone you know well (e.g., your child or a close friend).

Personalizing the topic Ⓡ

A Think about your own use of new media. Do you ever use two forms of media at once? Complete the following chart. One example is done for you.

ACTIVITY	What other forms of media do you use at the same time?
Doing homework	I listen to music or watch TV.
Watching television	
Listening to music	
Watching a movie or video	
Playing a computer game	
Sending an e-mail or text message	
Surfing the Internet	

B Compare charts with your classmates.

C With a group of classmates, discuss these two perspectives. Decide which you agree with.

- Using more than one form of media at once helps me to work better or to work faster.
- Using more than one form of media at once is distracting and has a negative effect on my work.

Reading 3

LEARNING AND THINKING WITH NEW MEDIA

New media in education

Technology has become an important part of education, particularly in expanding access to education. Many people go to school, find information, and do research on the Internet. They can download and read books, they can learn new skills by watching videos, and they
5 can communicate with others who have similar educational goals and interests.

Consider what takes place in a typical traditional classroom. A teacher presents information; the students study it and practice new skills they have learned. Students may also need to find additional
10 information outside of the classroom and present it to the teacher and their classmates. Technology can be useful in all of these activities: presenting, sharing, and finding information. Some teachers are using social media such as blogs, wikis, and YouTube in their classes. They say these new developments can improve education.

Social media – a distraction?

15 New media may offer advantages for education, but some people are concerned that technology can also be a distraction and may even get in the way of learning. For example, many university students bring their laptops to class so that they can take notes. However, this is not always exactly what happens. One professor at a U.S. university was
20 pleased to see her students working on their computers continuously during her class. However, as she walked around, she noticed that some students were also checking Facebook, sending instant messages, or surfing the Internet. She also noticed these students were not doing as well in her class. She decided to prohibit laptops in her classroom.
25 She is not alone in her concern. In 2010, an American university tried to block access to all social media for a week. The experiment did not work; most students found ways to access their e-mail and Facebook accounts anyway.

Some education professionals disagree with this effort to limit the
use of social media in education. They argue that teachers should not
fight against technology and that they should consider instead the
ways in which it can enhance education. For example, the students
in the class may have been sending instant messages to classmates in
order to explain something the professor said. Or they may have been
surfing the Internet to look up the definition of a word or to find more
information about a concept in the lecture.

Are new media changing how we think?

It is clear that the Internet is changing many aspects of our lives,
from communication to education. Some scholars believe it is also
changing how we think and learn, particularly in two areas: memory
and attention. A good memory has always been important for success
in school. In the past, students had to learn and remember a lot of
things – names of important people, lines of poems, mathematical
equations. Today, they can find these things instantly on the Internet
by looking them up on Wikipedia or doing a Google search. We don't
need to learn and remember them. In a way, the Internet has become
our collective memory.

Figure 6.4. Percentage of time multitasking

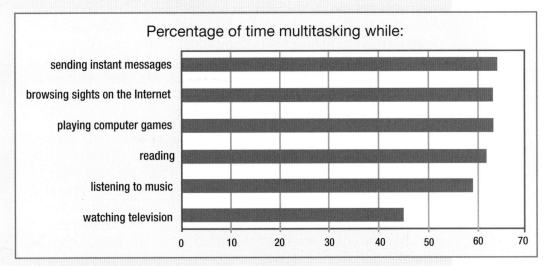

Percentage of time multitasking while:

Source: Kaiser Family Foundation

Regarding attention, one view is that before the Internet, we read and thought more deeply, with longer periods of concentration. With the immediate access and constant connection of the Internet, people 50 can get answers right away. Instead of reading a whole article, they read just a few sentences or paragraphs. They do not focus on one thing for very long. Traditional media have made changes in response to this new way of reading. Most newspapers now publish shorter articles. One of the most famous papers in the United States, the *New* 55 *York Times,* now provides short summaries of its most important stories on the second page so that readers do not need to read the longer articles.

New technology allows users to multitask; that is, they can do several different things at the same time. For example, students can ask 60 a librarian a question online while they are reading a Wikipedia entry and listening to music. Many people are proud of their multitasking skills, but is multitasking really a good strategy? In fact, several studies have shown that when we multitask, we do several things badly. A University of California study found that when people work at more 65 than one task at a time, they work faster but they produce less.

Multitasking is particularly common with new media. Young people, especially, often use several forms of media at once. They may listen to music, check their Facebook page, and play an online game, all at the same time. A 2010 study in England revealed that the average Briton spends seven hours a day using some form of media. However, the figure is closer to nine hours if you count the time that they spend on different forms of media at the same time. A 2006 study of young Americans found similar *media multitasking*. Almost 75 percent of the people in the study said that they sometimes use more than one form of media at the same time (see Figure 6.4).

Are these developments all bad? Some scholars and leaders believe that technology is making us stupid. We cannot pay attention to anything for very long. We learn and remember very little of importance. Opponents have a different perspective. They argue that the same thing was said about television, the printing press, and even the alphabet! They believe that the wide range and complexity of information makes us smarter, not dumber. It helps us learn to respond to multiple messages, to manage massive amounts of information, to make connections, and to decide what is important. These are exactly the skills that we will need as technology continues to develop and the amount of available information continues to expand. Just as tools, language, and literacy helped early human beings survive long ago, technology may help human beings survive into the future.

1 Answering multiple-choice questions Ⓐ Ⓡ

Many tests of reading comprehension are in multiple-choice format. Understanding strategies for answering can help you do better on this kind of test.

A Study the guidelines below for taking multiple-choice tests.

- Read the question and think about the answer before you look at the choices. One of them might match the answer you have thought of.
- Read the question and the directions carefully. Each question may be a little bit different.
- Read all the choices carefully before you decide.
- Cross out the choices that you know are wrong.
- If "all of the above" is one choice and you know that at least two statements are correct, then "all of the above" is probably the right answer.
- Read negative stems very carefully. They can trick you.
- A positive answer is more likely to be true than a negative answer.
- Answers with words like *never*, *always*, and *only* are often the wrong ones. Answers with words like *usually* and *often* are more likely to be the right one.
- The longest answer is often the right one.

B Answer the multiple-choice questions about the reading and the figure. Use the strategies in Step A to help you decide on the answers. Circle the correct answers.

1. According to the reading, what advantages can technology offer education?
   a. ways to share information, such as blogs and wikis
   b. ways to do research and find information
   c. ways to present information
   d. all of the above

2. Why did an American professor prohibit laptops in her classroom?
   a. She thought the students made too much noise.
   b. She thought that students were cheating.
   c. She thought students were doing things that were not related to her lecture.
   d. She could not see the students' faces.

3. According to the reading, which areas of thinking and learning may be affected by our use of new media? Circle all that apply.
   a. attention
   b. thought
   c. listening
   d. memory

4. Why did the *New York Times* start to publish summaries of its most important stories?
   a. There was not enough space in the newspaper.
   b. People read them before they read the longer stories.
   c. Most readers were multitasking.
   d. Reading behavior had changed for many people.

5. During which activity are young Americans most likely to multitask?
   a. sending instant messages
   b. reading
   c. sending e-mail
   d. watching television

6. According to the reading, what is an advantage of the expanded use of new media? Circle all that apply.
   a. Using new media will prepare us for the future.
   b. Media multitasking helps us pay attention.
   c. Using new media helps us manage information.
   d. Multimedia will increase our memories.

2 Guessing meaning from context Ⓥ Ⓡ

A Review the sentences from the text below. The paragraph numbers are in parentheses. Try to figure out the meaning of the boldface words from the context. Circle the correct choice.

1. They can download and read books, they can learn new skills by watching videos, and they can communicate with others who have similar educational **goals** and interests. (1)
   a. aims   b. ideas   c. tasks

2. They argue that teachers should not fight against technology and that they should consider instead the ways in which it can **enhance** education. (4)
   a. distract   b. increase   c. improve

3. Regarding attention, one view is that before the Internet, we read and thought more deeply, with longer periods of **concentration**. (6)
   a. lack of attention   b. deep thought   c. great skill

4. Many people are proud of their multitasking skills, but is multitasking really a good **strategy**? (7)
   a. plan   b. development   c. thought

5. Opponents have a different **perspective**. (9)
   a. idea   b. point of view   c. project

6. They believe that the wide range and **complexity** of information makes us smarter, not dumber. (9)
   a. unfamiliarity   b. great importance   c. difficult structure

7. These are exactly the skills that we will need as technology continues to develop and the amount of available information continues to **expand**. (9)
a. become more important   b. grow larger   c. become more complicated

8. Just as tools, language, and literacy helped early human beings survive long ago, technology may help human beings **survive** into the future. (9)
a. increase   b. earn more money   c. continue to exist

B What clues in the reading helped you figure out the meaning?

3 Preparing for an essay test Ⓐ Ⓡ Ⓦ

A With a group of classmates, consider the two perspectives presented in the reading as well as your discussion in the Preparing to Read task.

1. Our use of new media is making us stupid.

2. Our use of new media is preparing us for the future.

B Using information from the reading and your own experience, write down three pieces of information that support each perspective. Use full sentences.

1 _____

_____

_____

2 _____

_____

_____

C Decide which perspective you agree with. Find a classmate who has the opposite perspective and discuss your differences of opinion.

Chapter 6 Academic Vocabulary Review

The following words appear in the readings in Chapter 6. They all come from the Academic Word List, a list of words that researchers have discovered occur frequently in many different types of academic texts. For a complete list of all the Academic Word List words in this chapter and in all the readings in this book, see the Appendix on pages 213–214.

Reading 1 The Impact of the Internet on Mass Media	Reading 2 Social Media	Reading 3 Privacy and the Media
comments inaccessible integrated (adj) links medium (n) versions	finally interact location occur period revolution	equations lecture respond reveal strategy summaries

Complete the following sentences with words from the lists above.

1. For homework the students had to write short _Summary_ of their readings.
2. Taking notes is a good _strategy_ for remembering what you have read.
3. Visitors to the Web site can leave their _comments_ on the site's blog.
4. _Finally_, after a very long wait, someone answered the telephone.
5. You can click on the _links_ on the Web site to find out more information.
6. Devices like cellular phones and MP3 players have become _integrated_ into our lives.
7. The math teacher wrote a list of _equations_ on the board. The students reviewed them for their test.
8. New media allow users to _interact_ with one another online.
9. My favorite restaurant closed and moved to a new _location_ in another town.
10. Many changes _occur_ in the media in last half of the twentieth century.
11. Every few years there are new _versions_ of browsers such as Explorer and Firefox.
12. The president _respond_ to the journalists' questions.

Practicing Academic Writing

In this unit you have learned about the changing role of the media in society. For your writing assignment, you will first need to gather data from classmates, friends, and acquaintances.

Media Use

Develop a **survey** to find out how different groups get their news and entertainment and how they use the media for communication. Then write an essay based on your survey data to answer this question:

What are the most important factors that determine an individual's use of media? You may choose either of two areas to investigate:

(a) traditional media

(b) social media

PREPARING TO WRITE

A Choose *a* or *b*. Then, with a group of classmates, think about the material you have read in this unit and discuss the following questions. Your discussion will help you develop your survey.

- **a.** Traditional media: In reading 5.1, you considered the media choices of your classmates and your parents. What factors can explain the differences? Their ages? Their education? Other factors?

- **b.** Social media: Chapter 6 focused on new media, especially the rise of social media. What factors do you think can explain differences in the use of new media across the population? Users' ages? Their gender? Their jobs? The digital divide?

B With two or three classmates, write a survey of at least 10 questions. If you think the people who will take your survey are not proficient in English, you may write the survey in your first language.

Writing a Survey

Survey data can provide powerful information. However, the effectiveness of the survey depends on the quality of the questions. As you create your survey, be sure you write questions that will give you the information you want. For example, which of the following questions would provide better information?

- Do you use Facebook or another social networking site?   OR
- How often do you visit a social networking site?
  - Never
  - Once a week or less
  - Several times a week
  - Several times a day

The second option will give you more information. In general, it is better to use *Wh-* (who, what, when, how, why) questions than *Yes / No* questions in survey.

C In Step A you considered what factors might be important in media choices. You will write about these factors in your essay, so you will need to gather this information in your survey, as well. Be sure to include a place for people to provide information about themselves. A box like this one at the top of the survey is a good idea. You may want to add other factors.

Age ___   M ___ F___   Highest level of education _____

D Exchange surveys with another group of classmates and make any revisions based on their feedback.

E Now you will administer your survey. You may use your classmates' information, but you should also gather information from a wider and more diverse group of people. Each person in your group should give the survey to 10 people outside of your class.

F When you have collected all of your survey data, share the information with the other members of your group. Combine all of your responses. In other words, put all of the answers to Question 1 together, and so on.

G Based on all of the survey data, what kinds of generalizations can you make about media choices?

A Review the readings in the unit. Make notes on information you would like to include in your essay.

B Review the writing assignment in Chapter 5 on paraphrasing. Paraphrase any of the material you want to use in your essay.

C Review the assignment on introductory paragraphs from Chapter 3. Based on the generalizations you discovered in Step F, above, choose two for your main idea sentence. This sentence will make the central claims of your essay. Now complete the rest of the introductory paragraph. Be sure to include all three elements.

- Introduction of your topic – you may want to use your paraphrased information from the reading in your introduction.
- Your claim about the topic (your main idea sentence)
- Road map for the rest of your essay

D Review the writing assignment in Chapter 1 on body paragraphs. Now write two body paragraphs.

- Remember that every body paragraph should have a topic sentence. This sentence should state one of your generalizations.
- Be sure to provide evidence from your survey data for each of your generalizations.

AFTER YOU WRITE

Conclusions

Conclusions in short essays can be brief, but they should sum up what you have written. They should signal to the reader that the essay is ending.

A By now you should know what to look for when you revise your writing. Reread your draft and check that

- it has an introductory paragraph with a general statement and a main idea sentence that states your generalizations about media choices; and
- each body paragraph has a topic sentence and supporting evidence.

B Now look again at the end of your essay. It probably ends with the evidence for your second generalization. You can improve your essay by adding a few sentences of conclusion. Because your essay is short, you do not need to write a whole paragraph.

C Reread the two examples of conclusions from texts in Chapter 5. Notice that the concluding sentences refer to the main claim of the reading.

- The conclusion in reading 5.2 states that several factors contribute to the newsworthiness of a story.
- The conclusion in reading 5.3 refers to ethical decisions in publishing the news.

> 5.2 Often news reports are a combination of breaking news – events that have just happened – stories that satisfy our curiosity about important or famous people, and stories that touch us on a more emotional level.
> 5.3 Journalists and others in mass media must constantly balance the interests of the public with the confidentiality of personal and government information. The right choice is often not clear, and it is rarely easy to make.

D Notice, however, that these conclusions are not simply a repetition of the ideas in the introductory paragraph or the main idea sentence. The conclusion in reading 5.2 says it in a fresh, new way and refers to the most important factors in newsworthiness described in the text. The conclusion in reading 5.3 offers a comment about the difficulty of such decisions. As a result, the reading ends by putting us "in the journalists' shoes."

E Now write one or two sentences to conclude your essay.

F Exchange essays with a partner. Review his or her essay.

- Does it have an introductory paragraph with a general statement and a main idea sentence that reveals the two generalizations? Circle the two generalizations.
- If the essay contains information from other sources, has it been paraphrased?
- Does each body paragraph have a topic sentence? Underline them.
- Does the author provide enough evidence to support the generalizations in the essay?
- Does the author have a conclusion that is more than a repetition of the main idea?

G Revise your essay.

- Review your partner's suggestions.
- Review your own notes for revision.
- Make necessary changes.

H Edit your essay.

Read through your essay now for possible spelling mistakes, punctuation errors, subject-verb agreement errors, incorrect use of past tense, and article usage. Make corrections whenever you find errors.

Unit 4
Breaking the Rules

In this unit you will read about crime and society. In Chapter 7 the focus will be on crime and criminals: who commits crimes and why. You will also look how criminals have used technology. In Chapter 8 you will explore ways of preventing and controlling crime in society. You will look at technology again, this time how it has helped in the fight against crime. Finally, you will explore the ways in which society punishes those who commit crimes.

Contents

In Unit 4, you will read and write about the following topics.

Chapter 7 Crime and Criminals	Chapter 8 Controlling Crime
Reading 1 Deviance and Crime	**Reading 1** What Stops Us from Committing Crimes?
Reading 2 Who Commits Crimes?	**Reading 2** Science and Technology in Crime Fighting
Reading 3 Technology and Crime	**Reading 3** Crime and Punishments

Skills

In Unit 4, you will practice the following skills.

R Reading Skills	**W** Writing Skills
Thinking about the topic Scanning Understanding cartoons Reading critically Reading for main ideas Personalizing the topic Increasing reading speed Applying what you have read Reading for details	The passive voice Comparing data Going beyond the text Using data from a graphic Signals of chronological order Responding to prompts
V Vocabulary Skills	**A** Academic Success Skills
Words related to the topic Guessing meaning from context Synonyms Collocations Verbs of control Word families The Academic Word List	Answering short-answer test questions Highlighting Making a chart

Learning Outcomes

Write an essay based on a prompt

Previewing the Unit

> Before reading a unit (or chapter) of a textbook, it is a good idea to preview the contents page and think about the topics that will be covered. This will give you an overview of how the unit is organized and what it is going to be about.

Read the contents page for Unit 4 on page 162 and do the following activities.

Chapter 7: Crime and Criminals

A The first two readings in this chapter look at the kinds of crimes that commonly occur in most Western industrialized societies and who the criminals tend to be. Read each statement and circle the word you think makes it correct.

1. (More / Fewer) males are arrested for crimes than females.

2. Rich people are (more / less) likely to be arrested than poor people.

3. Younger people are (more / less) likely to be involved in crime than older people.

4. Property crimes like burglary are (more / less) common than violent crimes.

5. Homicide, or murder, is mostly committed by a (stranger / person) whom the victim knows.

6. Canada has a (higher / lower) annual murder rate than the United States.

B Review your answers after you have finished the first two readings in Chapter 7 to see if they were correct.

Chapter 8: Controlling Crime

A In this chapter you will read about what stops people from committing crimes, such as policing, and the punishment of people who break the law. Work in a small group. Think of five different kinds of punishment for criminals. For each kind of punishment, think of a type of crime that should receive this kind of punishment.

B Discuss the following question with your group: Are there any forms of punishment that should never be used?

Chapter 7
Crime and Criminals

1 Thinking about the topic Ⓡ

A Look up the meanings of *deviance* and *crime* in a dictionary.

B Work with a partner; Think about the relationship between deviance and crime. Discuss the following questions:

1. How would you define *deviant behavior*? You may wish to review Task 3, Expanded Definitions (Chapter 2, page 32). Write a definition beginning with:

   Deviant behavior is behavior that

2. How would you define *criminal behavior*? Write a definition, beginning with:

   Criminal behavior is behavior that

C Complete the table with behaviors that relate to the issues listed on the left.

Behaviors that are considered normal, deviant, or criminal in some societies			
Issue	**Normal**	**Deviant but not criminal**	**Deviant and criminal**
Use of the streets	Crossing the street at the traffic light		
Use of alcohol	Moderate social drinking		
Money	Working to earn money		

2 Words related to the topic Ⓥ

Work with a partner and describe these crimes and deviant behaviors. Look them up in a dictionary if you do not know them.

arms trafficking	assault	embezzlement	prostitution
arson	drug trafficking	gambling	tax evasion

Reading 1

DEVIANCE AND CRIME

Have you ever . . .

- driven through a stop sign without stopping?
- drunk or bought alcohol when you were below the legal age?
- taken something from a store without paying for it?
5   • cheated on a test?

If so, you have violated a socially accepted norm, or practice. In our society, this is considered *deviant behavior*. Deviant behavior is defined as behavior that is considered unacceptable, or outside the norms, for that society.

10   There are, of course, degrees of deviance, and not every member of a society will agree on what is deviant behavior and what is normal behavior. For example, although many people believe that prostitution is deviant, others see it as a legitimate way for people to earn a living. Also, what is seen as deviant behavior changes over time. Drinking 15 alcohol, for example, was regarded as unacceptable in the early twentieth century in the United States. It was illegal to sell, buy, or drink it. Today, drinking alcohol in moderation is accepted as normal social behavior for adults in the United States and in most Western countries.

20   What is considered to be deviant may also vary from place to place and from one culture to another. Although moderate drinking is acceptable in Western countries, in many Muslim countries, it is considered deviant. In many cultures, but certainly not in all cultures, it is regarded as deviant for a man to have more than one wife at the 25 same time. However, there are some religious groups and cultures where this practice is accepted.

Types of crime

Some acts of deviance may be regarded as simply unusual or rude whereas other deviant behaviors actually break the law. These behaviors are *crimes*. There are several categories of crimes. One 30 category is *violent crime*. These crimes include murder, rape, robbery, and assault. Violent crimes can sometimes also be *hate crimes*. In hate crimes, the victims are chosen because of their race, ethnicity, gender, national origin, or other personal characteristic. Another very common category is *property crime*, such as robbery, burglary, 35 or theft. In these crimes, there may be no physical harm to anyone. A robbery is when someone steals something directly from a victim, for example, on a street. A burglary is when someone enters a home or business illegally and steals something, but the victim may not even be there. Theft is like a burglary, but it does not involve illegal entry.

40   *Corporate crime*, or financial crime, is a different type of crime. Corporate crimes include tax evasion, embezzlement, and safety violations. Examples of safety violations would be the manufacture of a dangerous product or the creation of a big environmental problem. Finally, there is the category of *victimless crimes*. This term
45 is used because these crimes do not directly harm people other than the criminals themselves. Examples of victimless crimes include gambling, prostitution, and drug abuse. Of course, other people, such as the victims' families, may suffer indirectly from these "victimless" crimes.

50   We often think of crime as the act of a single person who wants to hurt another person or wants his or her money or property. However, crimes may sometimes be the work of a group of people working together. *Organized crime* usually has financial gain as its goal and it may operate across national borders. These criminal organizations
55 are involved in drug and arms trafficking, prostitution, gambling and other illegal activities. Many of them work very much like regular businesses. They are very powerful and dangerous.

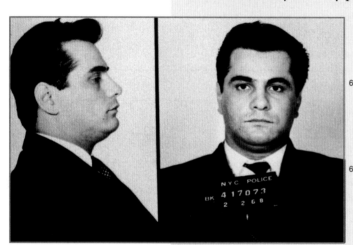

John Gotti, Jr., headed one of the biggest organized crime families in New York City.

Violent crimes

Murder, or *homicide*, is the most serious crime. It is also usually a personal
60 crime. Homicide is far more likely to be committed against acquaintances, friends, or relatives than against strangers. Homicide is usually a crime of passion; that is, it occurs when a
65 person feels uncontrollable emotions. Sometimes the person who commits a homicide feels that he or she has been mistreated. For example, a worker or student may become extremely angry if
70 he has been fired, or a student may lose control if she has been bullied. Recently, there has been an increase in workplace and school violence all over the world, in which workers or students take revenge for perceived mistreatment.

   Most people think that the *crime rate*, especially for violent crime, is rising. Crime rates vary considerably from one country to another
75 (see Figure 7.1), but in the United States, in fact, there has been a decline in the violent crime rate in the past 20 years. *Crime statistics*

School Shootings

In 2007, a student at a university called Virginia Tech in the United States killed 32 people and injured 17 others. Then he committed suicide. This was one of the deadliest school shootings in U.S. history. The student (see photo) had a history of mental health problems.

In 2002, a former student in Erfurt, Germany, shot and killed 18 people including students, teachers, and policemen and then committed suicide. He had been expelled from the school and was not allowed to take his university entrance examinations.

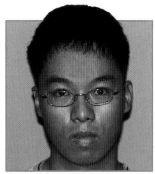

Virginia Tech shooter
Seung-hui Cho

should be interpreted with caution, however. First, although it is true that the violent crime rate has gone down, the number of these crimes has actually increased. The crime rate is the number of crimes per
80 person. Because the population has increased more quickly than the number of crimes, the crime rate has decreased. It should also be noted that these figures are based only on crimes that are reported. Many experts, including some police and government officials, believe that the real crime rate may be two or three times higher than these
85 figures.

Figure 7.1. Annual homicide rates by country per 100,000 people

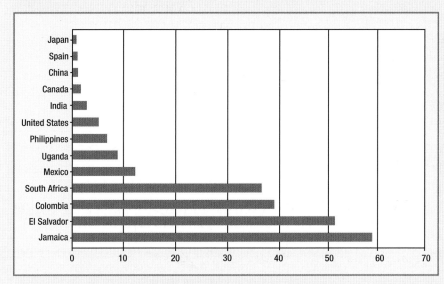

Source: United Nations (Most recent available figures for 2003–2008)

1 Scanning Ⓡ

Remember that scanning is looking quickly through a text to find a specific word or piece of information.

Scan the text and graphic material quickly to find the following. Write the answers.

1. a definition of hate crime _victim chose because of their race_

2. a definition of burglary _bussness illegaly ana steal_

3. examples of victimless crimes _prostitution, drugs_

4. the year of the Virginia Tech shooting _2007_

5. the countries with the highest and lowest annual homicide rates
Jamaica, Japan

2 The passive voice Ⓦ Ⓡ

In Chapter 2 you learned that writers use the passive voice when they want to focus on the person or thing that an action is happening to rather than the person or thing performing the action (the agent). The use of the passive is very common in academic writing and is used for other reasons as well.
The passive is also used when:

a. the agent is "people in general." This is common with verbs of thinking and feeling.

b. the author wants to avoid "giving orders" to the reader. In other words, the passive is more polite. In these cases, the passive often appears with *should.*

c. the author wants to continue using the same subject. It makes the writing flow better.

A Study the examples of these uses of the passive voice.

	Passive	Active
a	Gambling *is considered* deviant.	People *consider* gambling deviant.
b	It should *be recalled* that this was the original plan.	You should *recall* that this was the original plan.
c	**Many people** who commit crimes have had difficult lives. **They** may *have been abused or mistreated*.	**Many people** who commit crimes have had difficult lives. Someone *may have abused or mistreated* **them**.

B With a partner, find two examples of each type of passive use in the text. Highlight them.

Find use (a) in Paragraphs 1 through 4.

Find use (b) in Paragraph 8.

Find use (c) in Paragraph 7.

C Improve the sentences below by changing them to the passive voice.

1. In many Muslim countries, people regard drinking alcohol as deviant.

    In many Muslim contries drinking alcohol is regard as

2. The government considers travel to war zones dangerous.

    Travel to war zone is considered dangerous

3. Violent crimes in schools are increasing. Sometimes former students commit these crimes.

    Violent crimes in school sometime commited by former students

4. You should take this medicine with food.

    This medicine school be taken with food

5. People in some cultures accept prostitution as a legitimate profession.

    In some cultures prostitution is accepted as a legitemated proffesional

6. Victims of hate crimes suffer a lot because criminals select them on the basis of their race, gender, or ethnicity.

    Victims of hate crimes suffer a lot because they are selected

7. You should note that travel in these areas may be dangerous.

    It should be noted that travel in these area

8. We should protect children against violent crime.

    Children should be protected againt

3 Guessing meaning from context Ⓥ Ⓡ

Different kinds of context clues can help you figure out the approximate meanings of words. Sometimes the approximate meaning is good enough. You may not need to understand the exact meaning.

Context clues

- Explanations, synonyms, and examples
- Lists – If you know the meaning of other words in the list, you may be able to guess an unknown word.
- Contrast – If the sentences contain words that indicate contrast (for example, *although*, *however*, *but*) and you understand one side of the contrast, you may be able to guess the other side.

Use context clues in these sentences from the text to figure out the approximate meaning of the word in bold. The type of clue appears in brackets. Write the approximate meaning in the blank.

1. Although many people believe that prostitution is deviant, others see it as a **legitimate** way for people to earn a living. [contrast]

2. There are several **categories** of crimes. One category is . . . . Another very common category is . . . . [examples]

3. In hate crimes, the victims are chosen because of their race, **ethnicity**, gender, national origin, or other personal characteristic. [list]

4. Corporate crimes include tax evasion, embezzlement, and safety **violations**. Examples of safety violations would be the manufacture of a dangerous product or the creation of a big environmental problem. [examples]

5. Homicide is far more likely to be committed against **acquaintances**, friends, or relatives than against strangers. [list, contrast]

6. Sometimes the person who commits a homicide feels that he or she has been **mistreated**. For example, a worker who has been fired or a student who has been bullied may become extremely angry. [examples]
   treated badly

7. Homicide is usually a crime of **passion**; that is, it occurs when a person feels uncontrollable emotions. [definition]

8. Many **experts**, including some police and government officials, believe that the real crime rate may be two or three times higher than these figures. [examples]

4 Answering short-answer test questions Ⓐ Ⓦ

Write short answers to these test questions. Review Task 1 on page 168. Use information from "Deviance and Crime" in your answers.

1. According to the text, what is the difference between *deviance* and *crime*?

2. Why are some crimes considered "victimless"?

3. How does organized crime differ from crimes committed by individuals?

Understanding cartoons ®

Cartoons can often illustrate ideas more quickly and efficiently than words. This cartoon refers to "house arrest."
Criminals who are not considered violent or dangerous sometimes get a sentence of *house arrest*. This means they can live and work at home, but they cannot move freely anywhere else.

Study the cartoon and discuss the questions with a partner.

1. What do you think is this man's background?

2. What kind of crime do you think he committed?

3. Why is he asking about France, Bermuda, and Spain?

4. What is the artist trying to say about people like the criminal in the cartoon?

Reading 2

WHO COMMITS CRIME?

What kinds of people commit crimes and why? Crime statistics cannot give us a complete picture, but the information on reported crimes can give us some clues about the demographics of crime. If we consider all categories of crime together, the people who are most
5 likely to commit crimes are young men from lower socioeconomic backgrounds.

Age

Young people have the highest rates of arrest. One possible explanation is that older people gradually move away from crime. Or, they may become more skilled so they do not get caught as often. Experts
10 believe that younger people are more likely to get involved in crime because they have fewer relationships that encourage them to obey society's norms. A married person with children and a steady job is less likely to commit a crime than an unemployed, single, childless person.

Gender

15 In 2009, according to government reports, 77 percent of all those arrested in the United States were males. About 81 percent of the arrests for violent crime were men, but the figure for property crime arrests was much lower: 63 percent were men, and 37 percent were women. Although women commit all types of crime, they are most
20 likely to be involved in prostitution, theft, and shoplifting. They are less likely to be involved in violent crime or the more profitable crimes of burglary, robbery, and major corporate crimes. In other words, women are more likely to commit crimes that reflect their less powerful position in society. Most female criminals are unemployed,
25 uneducated, single mothers with small children.

Why are the figures for males and females so different? Sociologists suggest that it is more socially acceptable for males to be involved in crime than it is for females. If they do not conform to expected female roles and behaviors, they are more likely to be viewed negatively. It
30 has also been suggested that women have fewer opportunities to get involved in criminal behavior. Compared to males, potential female criminals are less likely to be accepted into criminal groups, they have a more limited range of criminal career paths open to them, and they have fewer opportunities for learning criminal skills. In other words,
35 like other employment opportunities, opportunities in crime are still much less available to women than to men.

A further argument is that in a male-dominated society, women are socialized differently from men. Consequently, women are less interested in achieving material success and more interested in the

40 emotional rewards that come from building close, personal relations with others. A desire for material success, it is argued, can lead people into crime if they lack other opportunities to gain such success.

Socioeconomic status

The majority of those arrested for violent and property crime is also from lower **socioeconomic groups**. Without money, it is harder to
45 keep out of trouble. It is also harder for poor people to hide their illegal behavior. They are more likely to use illegal drugs, for example, in a public place rather than in the safety of a comfortable home. As a result, they are more likely to get caught. In addition, poor people usually cannot afford to hire a lawyer to represent them if they do get
50 caught. In short, the poor are far more likely to get arrested. If they are arrested, they are more likely to be charged. If they are charged, they are more likely to be convicted, and if they are convicted, they are more likely to go to prison.

However, there is a whole category of crime – corporate crime –
55 that is usually committed by people of high social status who work as company officials. This is sometimes called *white-collar crime* because of the high social status of the people who commit such crimes. Examples of corporate crime include fraud and embezzlement, which involve dishonest and illegal financial activities. However, this category
60 also includes violations of safety regulations and environmental laws. Such crimes are committed without the obvious use of force, and it is difficult to show that the offender is responsible for the damage caused by the crime. For example, if a miner dies of lung disease, it is difficult
65 to show he died because the employer broke the law by not providing adequate safety in the mine. However, the harm caused by these activities is just as real as the harm caused by other types of crimes.

Compared to poor people who commit crimes, the
70 people who are involved in corporate crime often have a great deal of money and power that they use to avoid detection and conviction. As a result, many corporate criminals escape punishment. Finally, when corporate criminals are convicted, they often get much lighter
75 sentences than individuals who commit property and personal crimes.

The demographics of crime are complex, but there are clear patterns concerning who commits specific types of crimes, what kinds of criminals are mostly
80 likely to be caught, and what happens to them when they are convicted of their crimes.

socioeconomic group a group within a particular social structure, which depends on several factors, including occupation, education, and income

1 Reading critically Ⓡ

> Critical reading means you may need to find information that is not always directly
> or explicitly stated in the text. Sometimes you need to figure out for yourself the
> meaning that is suggested, or implied. Sometimes the authors show their views on
> a topic without actually stating them. Use what you know from your experience and
> from the text to answer questions about implied meanings.

The following questions are not answered directly in the text. Work with a partner to figure
out the answers.

1. According to the text, people with fewer social bonds are more likely to commit
   crimes. Do you think this is the only reason that unemployed people might commit
   a crime?

2. Why are corporate and financial crimes sometimes called "white-collar crimes?"

3. What do you think is the author's opinion about the connection between poverty
   and crime?

4. What do you think are the author's views on corporate crime?

2 Comparing data Ⓦ Ⓡ

> In academic writing it is common to compare one thing with another. When
> comparing data, you can often state the same information in different ways.

A State the comparisons below in a different way. Change the underlined words to their
opposite meaning and change other information as necessary. The first one is done as
an example.

Older   less   younger

1. ~~Younger~~ people are ~~more~~ likely to be involved in crime than ~~older~~ people.
   Older people are less likely to be involved in crime than younger people.

2. Younger people have <u>fewer</u> relationships that encourage them to follow conventional
   behavior than older people do.
   older people have more relanship that encorage them to follow

3. Women are <u>less</u> likely to be involved in the more profitable crimes of burglary and
   robbery than men are.
   men are more likely to be involed in the more protaboe

4. It is <u>more</u> socially acceptable for males to be involved in crime.
   It is less socially aceptable for famaies

5. Women are under <u>more</u> social pressure to conform than men.
   Men are onder less social pressure to conform

B The graph below shows information about the victims of violent crime in the United Kingdom in 2007. Write three sentences that compare facts that are shown in the graph.

Figure 7.2. Risk factors for violence

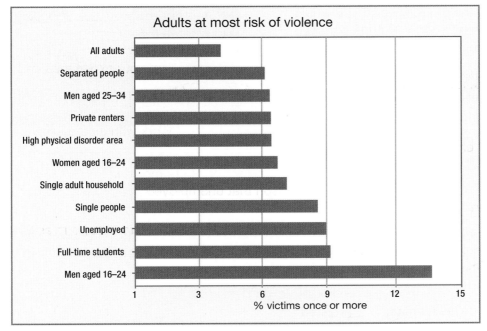

Source: United Kingdom Home Office

3 Words related to the topic V R

The reading contains many words related to crime.

A Cross out the word in the group below that has a meaning that is different from the other two.

offender   criminal

B With a partner, discuss the terms in the sentences below. If you do not know these words, look them up in a dictionary. Pay special attention to the prepositions that occur with the verbs. Put these seven actions in the order in which you would expect them to occur. Put the correct number from 1 through 7 in the blank.

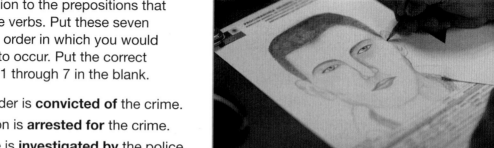

_6_ The offender is **convicted of** the crime.

_3_ The person is **arrested for** the crime.

_2_ The crime is **investigated by** the police.

_1_ A person **commits** a crime.

_7_ The offender is **sentenced to** time in prison.

_4_ The person is **charged with** the crime.

_5_ The person is **tried for** the crime.

C Read the true story of the serial killer, Thierry Paulin. Use the words in the box to fill in the blanks. In some cases, use your knowledge of collocations from Step B to help you choose. You will need to use some of the words more than once.

tried	**investigated**	**arrested**
charged	**sentenced**	**convicted**

Thierry Paulin was a serial killer in France in the 1980s. His first crime was in 1982. He robbed an elderly woman in a grocery store. He was _arrested_ for the crime a few days later, and he was _charged_ with robbery. He was _convicted_ of the crime and _sentenced_ to two years in prison. However, the sentence was suspended, which means he never had to spend any time in prison. He continued his life of crime, but his crimes became more serious. Between 1984 and 1987, he killed at least 18 elderly people and assaulted many others. The police _investigated_ these crimes, but Paulin did not leave much evidence when he attacked his victims. Finally, one of his victims survived, and she was able to describe Paulin to the police. Soon after, the police _arrested_ him and _charged_ him with several of the murders. However, he became very sick and died in prison in 1988 before he was _tried_ for these terrible crimes.

1 Thinking about the topic ®

A What kinds of crime are associated with computers? Work with a partner. Make a list of kinds of crime that involve computers.

_____

_____

_____

_____

B Compare lists with another pair of students.

2 Words related to the topic Ⓥ

A Discuss the meanings of the words with other students. Check an up-to-date dictionary if you are unsure. For the phrases, look up the word in bold.

computer **virus**
counterfeit products
cybercrime
fraud
hacking
identity **theft**
illegal **downloading**

B Tell your classmates about any cases of these crimes you know about. These could be famous cases in the news or experiences of a friend or an acquaintance.

TECHNOLOGY AND CRIME

In 1995, a U.S. government employee was arrested for stealing money from other employees' paychecks. Using the computer system, she took 10 cents from each of hundreds of thousands of these checks and deposited the money in her own account every month for nearly 12
5 years. In this way, she stole more than five million dollars. In another case, between 2005 and 2007, Albert Gonzalez sat at his computer in New Jersey, U.S.A., and using the Internet, stole over 130 million credit and bank machine card numbers all over the world. Then he used the numbers to withdraw money from bank machines and make
10 purchases worth millions of dollars.

Hacking

Advances in technology, especially the use of computers in business and in homes, have made these new kinds of crime possible. In 2008, one report estimated that the market for stolen data, such as credit card and bank account numbers, was worth 276 million dollars.
15 Criminals can pretend they are other people if they can get this personal information. This crime is called *identity theft*. Today, many people store personal data, such as birth dates and national identity numbers, on their computers, and they transmit information, such as passwords and credit card and bank account numbers, over the
20 Internet. It is possible for people like Gonzalez to *hack* into, or to break into, computer accounts illegally to steal this kind of personal information. Then they can open a new bank account, take out a loan, and even buy a house or a business, all in another person's name. In order to protect the privacy of personal information, it is important to
25 send it only by secure methods.

There are also other kinds of criminal activity on the Internet. For example, a company can set up a Web site and offer goods for sale, but the goods don't actually exist. A consumer may be tricked into sending money or credit card details to the company. Or the goods
30 for sale may be counterfeit. One American company that investigates businesses on the Internet estimates that about 20 percent of all brand-name goods on the Internet are fake products. Popular items include handbags, watches, software, and drugs. In 2009, the U. S. government received more than 330,000 complaints about this type of online *fraud*
35 with losses of almost $560 million.

Financial information is not the only goal for hacking and other kinds of **cybercrimes**. Some people want to cause harm to governments or other large organizations. The U.S. government reports that there were 1.8 billion cyber-attacks per month against
40 government agencies, including the White House and Congress, in 2010. The United States is not alone. There have been recent attempts to hack into the computers of the governments of Australia, India, Iran, and the Netherlands. Although many of these attempts to gain illegal entry may be carried out by young people for the thrill or the
45 challenge, others are serious attempts to steal information. Experts suspect that some hacking is organized by national governments.

Computer infections

Computer criminals can also cause harm in other ways. Computer viruses and worms are infectious computer programs that cause damage. Some of them rapidly reproduce, spreading to computers
50 all over the world. In 1999, the *Melissa* virus crippled Internet mail service around the world and caused an estimated $80 million of damage. When users opened an attachment in their e-mail, the virus began to damage their computers. In 2000, the *I Love You* worm used e-mail to reproduce, and it infected 50 million computers.

55 Computer-related crimes like these are growing at a rapid rate around the world, and the police are faced with a difficult job in preventing them. One challenge is that many computer crimes, especially thefts from companies, are not reported to the police. Although companies that are the victims of this kind of crime are
60 likely to suffer huge financial losses, they often keep quiet about it to protect their reputations. They do not want the public to think that they are vulnerable to such crimes because the public may lose confidence in the company. Another problem is that Internet crime has spread around the world.
65 The *I Love You* worm began in the Philippines but affected computers globally. Finding cybercriminals often requires international cooperation among
70 many different law enforcement agencies. Finally, it is difficult for police to keep up with the necessary technological skills. They need special training and
75 expensive equipment to fight computer crime effectively.

cybercrime
a crime that is committed with the help of computers and/or the Internet

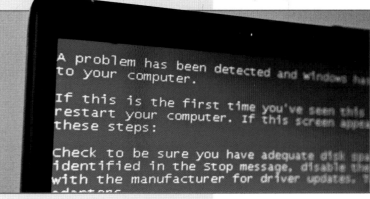

Viruses can seriously damage computers.

Computer technology and ethics

Many of these crimes are so new that the public does not know what to think of them. A recent study found that one in every six people in the United States believes that traditional ideas of right and wrong have been changed by new technologies. Most people do not hack into other people's computers, but they may engage in less serious illegal behavior. For example, people who would never steal anything from a store might illegally download and share music, movies, and television shows. One organization estimated that over 40 billion songs were illegally downloaded or shared worldwide in 2008. It estimates that only between 5 and 10 percent of all music downloads are legal. The estimate for legal video downloads is also only about 15 percent. Some television programs are copied illegally more often than they are viewed on television! Many people don't believe these activities are wrong, and they don't know they are illegal. Computer technology makes it easier for both ordinary people and criminals to break the law.

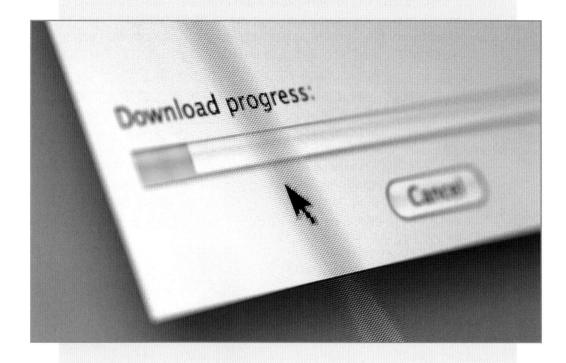

1 Reading for main ideas ®

Look back at the text to find which part expresses each main idea below. Write the paragraph number next to the main idea.

___ **a.** Some criminals use computers to steal personal information.

___ **b.** There have been numerous cyber-attacks against national governments.

___ **c.** Computer viruses and worms can cause considerable damage.

___ **d.** Technology may have changed the public's attitude about some crimes.

___ **e.** Computer technology has led to some spectacular financial crimes.

___ **f.** Some companies have used the Internet to commit fraud.

___ **g.** It is difficult for law enforcement to fight cybercrime.

2 Synonyms Ⓥ Ⓡ

> In some pairs of synonyms, one word in the pair is more specialized and the other is more general. In academic texts, authors often try to use more specialized terms in order to vary their language. For example, in (1), *deposit* and *put in* are synonyms, but *deposit* is the more specialized term. It is often related to money.

A The vocabulary items in the list below are relatively common. There are words and phrases in the text that have a similar meaning but are less common. Find them and write them on the lines below.

1. put in (Par. 1)   *deposit* _____

2. take out (Par. 1)   _____

3. buy (Par. 1)   _____

4. information (Par. 2)   _____

5. send (Par. 2)   _____

6. safe (Par. 2)   _____

7. fake (Par. 3)   _____

8. believe something is true (Par. 4) _____

9. agencies (Par. 4)   _____

10. fast (Par. 5)   _____

B Read the sentences with the boldface words. Then discuss with your classmates which is a more likely conclusion, *a* or *b*.

1. His mother **suspected** he had been smoking.
   a. She smelled smoke on his clothes.   b. She saw him with a cigarette.

2. He decided to **withdraw** $600 to pay for his computer.
   a. He went to the computer store.   b. He went to the bank.

3. The students gathered economic **data** about different countries for their project.
   a. They went to the library.   b. They asked their parents.

4. In the United States, government **agencies** are closed on Sundays.
   a. The Post Office and passport office are closed on Sundays.
   b. The White House is closed on Sundays.

5. She **deposited** her paycheck yesterday.
   a. The amount in her bank account is larger today.
   b. The amount in her bank account is smaller today.

6. The police found a large supply of **counterfeit** watches.
   a. The police are going to buy the watches.
   b. The police are going to destroy the watches.

7. The computer in the company's main office **transmits** information about products to their other offices.
   a. Managers in all of the offices have up-to-date information.
   b. The managers in all of the offices only want the most important information.

8. She **made** so many **purchases** that she had to take a taxi home.
   a. Her bags were heavy.   b. The taxi was expensive.

9. We have to move the equipment inside **rapidly**. A storm is coming.
   a. The storm will bring heavy rain and wind tomorrow.
   b. The storm is very close.

10. She keeps all of her important papers in a **secure** location.
    a. Her papers are in a locked box.   b. Her papers are in another country.

3 Collocations Ⓥ Ⓡ

You have learned that some verbs typically collocate with specific nouns and others collocate with specific prepositions. In addition, some collocate with a noun *and* a preposition in the same phrase.

A The verbs on the list appear in the text. Scan the text to find the nouns and prepositions that collocate with them. The paragraph numbers can help you locate them. In each box in the chart with a dot (•), write the appropriate word from the text. The first has been done for you.

	Collocation with Noun	Collocation with Preposition	Collocation with Both a Noun and a Preposition
break (Line 21)		• break into	
take (Line 22)		•	•
trick (Line 28)		•	
gain (Lines 43–44)	•		
be faced (Line 56)		•	
suffer (Line 60)	•		
lose (Lines 62–63)	•		•
engage (Line 81)			•
break (Line 93)	•		

B Use your knowledge of collocations to fill in the correct verbs. The collocating words are in bold.

1. Two older children _____ the little boy **into** giving them his candy.

2. Many computer companies _____ big **losses** during the 1990s.

3. The country _____ **with** serious economic challenges.

4. Burglars _____ **into** our house while we were on vacation.

5. People who _____ **in** some kinds of deviant **behavior** are considered criminals.

6. Adults who _____ **the law** usually get a more serious punishment than do teenagers who commit similar crimes.

7. Many citizens _____ **confidence in** the government after the earthquake.

8. The burglars were able to _____ **entry** through a back window.

9. The young couple went to the bank to _____ **out a loan** for their new house.

4 Going beyond the text Ⓦ Ⓡ

A Find out what your classmates think about the topic of technology and ethics. Make sure there is a response from everyone in the class. Keep a record of the answers. Use this scale:

1	2	3	4	5
Strongly agree	Agree	Not sure	Disagree	Strongly disagree

1. It is acceptable to download music from the Internet without paying for it.

   1   2   3   4   5

2. It is acceptable share music files with other people.

   1   2   3   4   5

3. It is acceptable to download or watch television programs or movies without paying for them if they are available on the Internet.

   1   2   3   4   5

4. It is acceptable to use someone else's wireless connection without permission.

   1   2   3   4   5

5. It is acceptable to copy software at your office or school and use it at home.

   1   2   3   4   5

6. It is acceptable to use computers at your office for personal business, such as e-mail or shopping.

   1   2   3   4   5

B Combine your results so that you have one set of answers for each question. For example:

It is acceptable to download music from the Internet without paying for it.

50%	15%	5%	5%	0%
Strongly agree	Agree	Not sure	Disagree	Strongly disagree

C Write up your findings in a short paragraph.

D With your classmates, discuss possible reasons for your findings.

Chapter 7 Academic Vocabulary Review

The following words appear in the readings in Chapter 7. They all come from the Academic Word List, a list of words that researchers have discovered occur frequently in many different types of academic texts. For a complete list of all the Academic Word List words in this chapter and in all the readings in this book, see the Appendix on pages 213–214.

Reading 1 Deviance and Crime	Reading 2 Who Commits Crimes?	Reading 3 Technology and Crime
corporate decline (n) financial founder mental statistics	adequate individuals obvious potential (adj) regulations status	attachment challenge equipment estimate (v) items methods

Complete the sentences with words from the lists.

1. I left several important _____ in my office. I need to go pick them up.

2. When the _____ of the company died, his children sold it to its current owner.

3. Business owners must follow many government rules and _____ .

4. The government _____ that that the economy grew at about 2 percent last year.

5. Cybercrime presents the police with a significant _____ . Sometimes criminals have better technology than they do.

6. The mayor reported this year's _____ on violent crime. They showed an increase in violent crime among people between the ages of 18 and 21.

7. There was a _____ in violent crime last year, but property crimes increased.

8. The city bought modern _____ for its police department to help them solve more crimes.

9. When they examined the company's _____ records, they discovered illegal activity.

10. It was _____ that the two students cheated on their test. They had the same answers.

11. _____ health is just as important as physical health.

12. The police use many different _____ to solve crimes.

Developing Writing Skills

Assignments and tests in many academic courses require you to write an essay in response to a *prompt*. On tests, essay questions are often the most difficult types of questions to answer, but you can prepare for them. These guidelines can help you.

Responding to prompts

Before a test:

1. Keep up with your reading.
2. Take notes on readings and lectures.
3. Review your notes.
4. Try to predict what the essay questions will be.
5. For writing assignments or for an essay question on a test, read the prompt carefully. Be sure you understand what the question is asking. Pay special attention to the verb in the question. Here are some examples of prompt types. (*X* is the topic you're writing about.)

   - *Explain X* – Tell about the ways in which X is complicated. Make X as clear and understandable as possible for the reader.
   - *Discuss X* – Consider all the different elements of X. This is probably the broadest of all essay question types.
   - *Evaluate X* – Discuss the significance or validity of X.
   - *Illustrate X* – Give examples of X with details.
   - *Compare X and Y* – Give points of similarity and difference between two or more things.
   - *Describe X* – Explain all of the features of X in a logical sequence.
   - *Analyze X* – Divide X into parts and discuss each of these parts and how they are related to the whole X.

6. Plan your time.
7. Outline your answer briefly or make some notes before you begin to write.

A Review the guidelines in the box with a partner.

B The following prompts refer to material in this chapter. Use the guidelines from the box to help you. With a partner, discuss how you would answer each of them. Make notes or a brief outline to show how you would respond. The first is done as an example.

1. Discuss reasons for workplace and school violence.

   <u>What is wkpl viol? Recent increase</u>

   <u>Economic probs, availability of guns</u>

2. Explain the relationship between socioeconomic status and crime.

   _____

   _____

3. Compare the crime profiles of men and women.

   _____

   _____

4. Evaluate the term "victimless crime."

   _____

   _____

5. Describe how a person may become a victim of identity theft.

   _____

   _____

C Choose two prompts and respond to them in a one-paragraph answer. Or, work with prompts assigned by your teacher. Use the notes that you made with your partner in Step B.

D Exchange paragraphs with your classmate. Did he or she follow the guidelines for responding to prompts?

E Use what you have learned to predict three essay questions for any of the readings in this text.

Chapter 8
Controlling Crime

1 Personalizing the topic ®

Some of the reasons people do not break the law are:
  a. They have a strong moral belief that it is wrong.
  b. They think that their families and friends would disapprove.
  c. They might have to pay a fine if they are caught.
  d. They are afraid they might have to go to prison.

A Which, if any, of the reasons above would stop you from doing the following things? Put a check mark (✓) next to all that apply.

___ **1.** parking illegally

___ **2.** copying computer software illegally

___ **3.** driving too fast

___ **4.** smoking in public places where it is prohibited

___ **5.** buying illegal copies of movies or computer games

___ **6.** not paying taxes

B Compare answers with a partner.

2 Increasing reading speed ®

When you practice speed-reading techniques, you should use these reading strategies:
  • Do not say the words under your breath as you read.
  • Focus on groups of words, not individual words.
  • Do not backtrack (go over the text again and again).
  • Guess at the general meaning of words that you do not know.
  • Skip over words that you do not know and that do not seem too important.
  • Slow down slightly for key information, such as definitions and main ideas.
  • Speed up for less important information, such as examples and details.

Practice speed-reading techniques as you read "What Stops Us from Committing Crimes?" Time yourself (or your teacher will time you).

Reading 1

WHAT STOPS US FROM COMMITTING CRIMES?

If a society is to continue to function smoothly, then the members of that society need to behave in orderly ways: They need to conform to certain norms and obey certain rules. Why do most people in a society agree to obey the rules? According to sociologists, there are
5 two kinds of controls that influence the way an individual behaves. These are referred to as *internal controls* and *external controls*.

Internal controls

Imagine you are in a bookstore and you see a book that you want. You do not have enough money to pay for it, but the thought of stealing the book does not occur to you. Why not? The answer is internal
10 controls. Internal controls are the controls that you impose on yourself based on your values, beliefs, and fears. You develop these values, beliefs, and fears as a result of socialization into your particular community.

One of these values is that stealing is wrong.
15 To continue to feel good about yourself, you don't steal. So the first aspect of internal control is your *self-image*, or how you see yourself. The second aspect of internal control is the possible disapproval of friends and family who might find
20 out about your shoplifting. You do not want to have to talk with your parents, husband or wife, or friends about why you stole a book. The third factor that may deter you from stealing is the fear of detection and its consequences. You probably do
25 not want to be arrested. Many shops display signs that say shoplifters will be reported and prosecuted. Some stores also employ detectives to discourage shoppers from stealing and to identify those who do steal. They know that fear of arrest is an effective
30 form of control.

Shoplifters will be prosecuted

Finally, your social and economic circumstances, such as whether you are employed full time, may influence whether you steal or not. You may be afraid of other consequences, such as losing your job or losing the trust
35 of your colleagues. In a study of property crime arrests, researchers compared the percentage of arrests in two populations: people with full-time jobs and people who were not employed. The researchers found that the percentage of arrests among those who were not employed was much higher. One theory in sociology states that our
40 internal controls develop out of the *social bonds*, such as employment,

friendships, and family, that connect people in a community. Deviance tends to occur when these social bonds are weak. Strong bonds make deviant behavior a less attractive choice.

External controls

For some individuals, internal controls are not enough to stop them
45 from breaking the law. For these people, the imposition of external controls, such as policing and punishment, may discourage them from committing crimes. Some controls, such as policing and closed circuit cameras, are preventive. If you see a police car at the corner, you probably will not drive through a red light. If you see a camera in
50 a store, you are not likely to shoplift.

Other external controls are punishments for deviant behavior. There are three main kinds of these punitive external controls. The least serious form is public shaming. More serious is the payment of fines or the loss of some privilege such as the right to drive. Finally,
55 the most severe is imprisonment, and in some societies, physical punishment or even death. Consider the driving example. If a police officer stopped you for driving too fast, you would probably be embarrassed as other passing drivers stared at you. If you were driving at a very high speed, you would probably also have to pay a fine. If you
60 were driving while drunk, you could also lose your driver's license, or you might even have to serve time in prison.

There are a number of factors in the effectiveness of these external controls in stopping people from committing crimes. Their effectiveness depends, in part, on the certainty of punishment. If
65 there is little likelihood of being caught, the external controls may not be very effective deterrents. It also depends on the severity of the punishment. The threat of prison is more likely to prevent people from breaking the law than the threat of a small fine. For some crimes, however, even very strong external controls do not seem to be very
70 effective. For example, people who commit "crimes of passion" feel uncontrollable rage or overwhelming emotional pressure. They may not give any consideration to the consequences of their actions. In this type of crime, both internal and external controls fail. Under normal circumstances, and in most societies, however, the combination of
75 internal and external controls results in conformity to accepted norms and the prevention of many crimes.

1 Highlighting Ⓐ Ⓡ

> Remember that highlighting sections of a text is a useful way to begin making notes from a text.

Find and highlight the following in the text:

- definition of internal controls
- four aspects of internal controls
- two types external controls
- three examples of punitive external controls

2 Verbs of control Ⓥ Ⓦ

> Some verbs are especially useful in describing internal and external controls on behavior.
> They are commonly used in a pattern like the ones in the chart below. Notice the use of the preposition *from* in the second column and the use of the *-ing* form of the verb in the third column.
>
> | | Control verb + noun phrase *from* | *-ing* form |
> | --- | --- | --- |
> | A fear of + noun phrase
The threat of + noun phrase
The thought of + noun phrase | discourages someone from
deters someone from
prevents someone from
stops someone from | breaking the law
speeding
cheating on a test
committing a crime |
>
> Different types of noun phrases can fit in the first column.
> Examples:
> *The thought of* **my parents' anger** *stops me from behaving badly.*
> *A fear of* **getting caught** *stops me from shoplifting.*

A Scan the text to find instances of these control verbs.

- deter (Par. 3) *deter you from stealing*
- discourage (Pars. 3 and 5) *discourage them from commiting crimes*
- prevent (Par. 7) *prevent people from breaking the law*
- stop (Par. 5) *stop them from breaking the law*

B Use the pattern in the chart to write three sentences of your own.

- stop everyone from cheating on a exam
- prevents my frend from lying her mom
- discorage someone from commiting a crime

3 Word families Ⓥ Ⓡ

> The verbs from Task 2 and other verbs of control have noun and adjective forms as well.

A Scan the text to find other forms of the verbs in the chart. Write the forms in the open boxes.

Paragraph	VERB	NOUN	ADJECTIVE
7	conform	conformity	
3	detect	detection	
7	deter	deterrence	
3	disapprove	disaproval	
5	impose	imposition	
7	prevent	prevention	preventive
5, 6	punish	punishment	punitive

B You can expand your active vocabulary by learning other forms of new words that you learn. Find the noun forms for the verbs from the reading in the chart below. Find adjective forms for open boxes.

VERB	NOUN	ADJECTIVE
discourage	discouragement	
influence	influence	influential
obey	obediance	obedient
prosecute	prosecution	
shame	shame	shameful

C Write sentences with three of the new forms you wrote in the chart in Step B.

4 Applying what you have read Ⓡ

> As a college student, one of the things you must not do is to copy someone else's work and present it as your own. This is called *plagiarism.*

Discuss with other students:

1. What internal controls discourage you from plagiarizing?
2. What external controls exist to prevent plagiarism? (Find out if your school or college has rules about plagiarism and, if so, what they are.)

Thinking about the topic ℝ

One way to activate your background knowledge before you start reading is to brainstorm. When you brainstorm, you try to think of as many ideas as you can. You do not try to evaluate or organize your ideas; you just quickly make a list.

Think of television programs and movies you have seen about detectives solving crimes. Use those memories and the pictures below to do the following task.

1. Work in a small group. For five minutes, brainstorm different ways to solve crimes. Make a list.
2. Compare your list with another group's list.
3. In the text "Science and Technology in Crime Fighting," one of the methods of crime detection discussed involves the use of DNA. Read the following description of DNA.

   DNA stands for *deoxyribonucleic acid.* These are the molecules that make up the chromosomes that are a part of every cell in our bodies. Everyone (except identical twins) has a different DNA code.

4. Discuss with a partner how you think DNA might be useful in solving crime.

Reading 2

SCIENCE AND TECHNOLOGY IN CRIME FIGHTING

law enforcement agencies
government offices that are responsible for upholding laws and finding people who break them

Even effective controls cannot prevent all crimes. Therefore, when crimes do occur, society must have a way to find out who has committed them. The first step in enforcing the law is detection, in other words, solving the crime. **Law enforcement agencies** have been
5 working to solve crimes for many years. It is a challenging job, but in recent history, *forensics* – the use of science and technology to solve crimes – has become an important tool.

Fingerprints

Probably the most important advance in forensics in the past century is the widespread use of fingerprints for identification. A person's
10 fingerprints are the swirled patterns on the skin at the tips of the fingers. These patterns do not change over time, and they can be used to identify people. Fingerprints are made when someone touches a surface. Sweat and acids from the body transfer to the surface and leave a mark. Sometimes it is only a partial fingerprint, but that can
15 be sufficient to make an identification. Many fingerprints are invisible under normal circumstances, but they can be made visible with special chemicals. Prints can also be examined in darkness using high-powered lasers, and they can be retrieved from almost any surface – even clothing, plastic bags, or human skin.

20　　Law enforcement agencies all over the world have large collections of fingerprints to aid in crime detection. These have been computerized to make it easier to search for matching prints. If fingerprints are found at a crime scene, they can be compared with the fingerprints stored in a computer bank. However, fingerprint matching is not as
25 reliable as many people believe. For a long time, it was believed that everyone had a unique set of fingerprints. Experts are still debating this claim, but one thing is clear: both people and machines can make mistakes. In 2004, a lawyer in Oregon was arrested for participation in the bombing of a train in Madrid based on a fingerprint. It was later
30 discovered the match was a mistake. Mistakes like this can ruin the lives of innocent people.

Words, blood, and insects

Law enforcement has used other forms of
technology to help solve crimes. These include
the analysis of handwriting to find the author of
a document. Most people have their own way
of writing letters, which a trained professional
can recognize. Handwriting analysis has been
used to identify a wide range of offenders, from
serial killers to *war criminals*. Bloodstains are
also important clues in violent crimes. Criminals
sometimes try to wash blood away, but forensic
professionals can detect blood even if the ratio
of blood to water is 1:12,000. The patterns of the
bloodstains also provide information about the
crime. When a drop of blood hits a flat surface,
the shape of the drop can reveal how far and
how fast it has fallen. Drops that travel a short
distance are big and round. Blood that falls with
greater force forms smaller drops (see photos).
Some other forensic techniques are more
surprising. Scientists can sometimes use insects
to help solve murder cases. They can estimate
the time of a victim's death by measuring how
long it takes the insects to break down body tissue. Insects can also
help solve drug crimes. They are often found in illegal shipments
of drugs. If detectives know where the insects come from, they can
trace the drugs back to a particular location in the world.

DNA

The most important recent development in forensic science is the use
of DNA for identification. DNA analysis is based on the fact that every
person (except an identical twin) has unique DNA. A sample of DNA
can be taken from a person and matched to a sample of DNA taken
from a crime scene – from a drop of blood, saliva, or perhaps a strand
of hair. Then computers can search for matches to the sample. For
example, if the police arrest a murder suspect, they might give him a
cup of coffee while they are questioning him. After the suspect leaves
the room, they can take his coffee cup. The saliva on the cup contains
his DNA. If tests show that his DNA matches DNA at the crime scene,
this is strong evidence for their case.

However, DNA analysis is controversial. On the one hand, it helps
70 police to find criminals and prove that they are guilty. In addition,
DNA evidence can also help innocent people. If there is no match
to DNA from the crime scene, suspects can be eliminated. So, most
people see DNA analysis as a positive technological advancement. On
the other hand, some people see it as a serious invasion of privacy,
75 like a police search of a person or place without their permission.
According to United States law, DNA is seen as similar to other
"property" that someone has abandoned. If a suspect leaves saliva on
a glass in a restaurant, or a cigarette on a sidewalk, this is abandoned
property, and the police may use it as evidence. Fingerprinting and
80 DNA analysis are good examples of how science and technology are
transforming crime fighting but also creating new questions.

Table 8.1. Common DNA Evidence

Evidence	Possible Location of DNA	Source of DNA
Hat or scarf	inside surfaces	hair, skin, sweat, blood
Eyeglasses	nose- and earpieces, lenses	sweat, skin
Used cigarette	butt	saliva
Used envelope	inside flap	saliva
Bottle, can, or glass	mouthpiece	saliva, sweat, skin
Bed sheets	surfaces	blood, sweat, hair
Fingernails	scrapings from underneath nails	blood, skin

Source: U.S. Dept. of Justice.

Finding Mengele

In 1979 an old man drowned in Brazil. Six
years later, handwriting experts in Brazil and
Germany confirmed that the handwriting in
letters and other documents that were found
in the house where the old man lived matched
the handwriting of Nazi war criminal, Josef
Mengele. International authorities had been
searching for Mengele for 40 years.

1 Reading for details ®

A Review the guidelines for answering multiple-choice questions on page 153 and true/false questions on page 128.

B Circle the correct answer according to what you have read in the text.

1. Why are fingerprints so important in the detection of crimes?
   a. There are fingerprints at every crime scene.
   b. Fingerprints can help identify the person who committed the crime.
   c. Every person's fingerprints are different.
   d. all of the above

2. Fingerprint matches are always correct.
   a. True
   b. False

3. Why is the analysis of blood useful in crime detection?
   a. The shape of the blood drops can provide clues about the crime.
   b. Blood contains DNA, which could identify people at the crime scene.
   c. It is almost impossible to wash all of the blood away.
   d. all of the above

4. How can insects help in crime detection? Circle all that apply.
   a. Their DNA is used in the analysis of crime scenes.
   b. Law enforcement agencies can use them to find the origin of shipments.
   c. Insects can help detectives determine the time of death.
   d. Each insect is unique and can provide evidence of a crime.

5. Saliva often contains enough DNA to identify a suspect.
   a. True
   b. False

6. Why is DNA analysis controversial?
   a. Sometimes the police make mistakes in DNA identification.
   b. Some people think DNA testing is illegal.
   c. Police cannot always get enough DNA to make an identification.
   d. all of the above

2 Using data from a graphic Ⓦ Ⓡ

> Some assignments will require you to write based on information in graphs, charts, or tables.

A Complete the following sentences, using information from the "Common DNA Evidence" table on page 196.

1. Hair is a useful source of DNA. It is sometimes found on _Hat_____ .
2. Detectives often find DNA from _Saliva_____ , _sweat_____ , or _skin_____ on bottles and cans.
3. DNA evidence is can be found on small items such as _fingertips_____ as well as larger items, such as _cigarette_____ .
4. Police may scrape under a victim's fingernails to obtain _blood_____ or _skin_____ .

B Write two more sentences of your own using information in the table.

3 The Academic Word List Ⓥ

A Match the words from the text in the left-hand column to their meanings in the right-hand column. Write the letters of the words in the blanks.

_h_ **1.** occur	**a.** not the same as anything else
_f_ **2.** enforcement	**b.** remove or take away
_i_ **3.** visible	**c.** found the origin of something
_a_ **4.** unique	**d.** left something forever
_j_ **5.** debated	**e.** change completely
_l_ **6.** ratio	**f.** a way of making people obey the law
_c_ **7.** traced	**g.** exactly the same
_g_ **8.** identical	**h.** happen
_k_ **9.** controversial	**i.** possible to see
_b_ **10.** eliminate	**j.** argued
_d_ **11.** abandoned	**k.** causing disagreement
_e_ **12.** transform	**l.** the size of one thing as compared to another

B Complete the sentences with the 12 AWL words from Step A. Do not change the form of the word. Use each word only once.

1. Some crime fighting methods are _controversial_ . Not everybody agrees that they are fair.
2. The criminal _abandoned_ his car on an empty road and ran into the woods.
3. Crimes _occur_ in every community. They are part of the human experience.
4. The police _traced_ the victim's family back to a small village in Spain.
5. Even with the best technology, we will probably never _eliminated_ all crime.
6. I cannot tell the difference between these two photographs. They look _identical_ to me.
7. She tried to see the people across the street but no one was _visible_ in the darkness.
8. Even small amounts of money can sometimes _transform_ poor communities into comfortable places to live.
9. The student to teacher _ratio_ in this school is 25:1.
10. For many years, the state of Nevada was _unique_ in the United States. It was the only state that allowed gambling.
11. The police are responsible for the _enforcement_ of the city's laws.
12. The committee members _debated_ several different ways to raise money for the school music program, but they could not come to a decision.

4 Signals of chronological order Ⓦ Ⓡ

Academic texts often include passages that tell about a sequence of events. This could be a story, or it could be an account of how someone conducted an experiment or a piece of research. These events are told in the order in which they happened, that is, in *chronological* order. Words such as *then*, *later*, *after*, and *while* are used to help you keep track of the sequence of the events.

A Read this paragraph that tells more about how some New York City police officers solved a crime. Underline the words that indicate time. The first one is done for you.

When the New York City police arrested a murder suspect in June 1998, they had no evidence connecting him to the crime. A few days later they were able to connect him to that homicide, plus two others – and it all came down to a cup of coffee. The man, who had been arrested on a theft charge, was given coffee by detectives while they were questioning him. After the suspect left the room, the detectives sent the cup to a lab for analysis. The lab obtained his DNA from the saliva he left on the cup. Testing then showed that his DNA matched not only the DNA found at the scene of the original murder but DNA from other crimes as well.

B Answer the following questions:

1. Which words indicate that two events occurred at the same time?

_____

_____

2. Which words indicate that the events occurred in a sequence?

_____

_____

_____

C Imagine that you are a detective. You have been involved in solving a crime using DNA. It could be a property crime or a violent crime. Now you must write up your report in one or two paragraphs. Tell the story of how you collected the DNA and how it helped you to find the criminal. Use the guide questions below to help you get started. Be sure to use signals of chronological order to make clear the sequence of your actions. The information in this section and in previous readings in this chapter will provide ideas.

1. What was the crime?

2. Who was the suspect?

3. How did you collect the DNA?

4. Then what happened?

1 Personalizing the topic ®

Discuss with a small group:

1. Have you ever visited a prison? If so, where? What was it like? If not, what do you imagine a prison to be like?
2. Are there different types of prisons in your country? What are they?
3. Do prisons in your country try to rehabilitate prisoners, that is, prepare them for a normal, useful life after prison?
4. In your country, can people be let out of prison early for good behavior?

2 Thinking about the topic ®

The following statistics show prison terms in the United States.

Mean Sentence Length by Offense Type in U.S. State Prisons in 2008

Type of offense	Percentage of all offenses	Mean sentence length in months
Violent offenses	28.3	93
Property offenses	27.1	49
Drug offenses	28.4	56
Public disorder	15.6	48

Source: U.S. Bureau of Justice Statistics

A Work with a partner and analyze the information in the table. Make three statements about the information. For example:

> According to the information in the table, there are about the same number of violent and property offenses.

B Does any of the information in this table surprise you? Why or why not? Discuss with your partner.

Reading 3

CRIME AND PUNISHMENT

The purpose of external controls is to prevent deviant behavior, but they do not always work. When a crime does occur, law enforcement – detection and prosecution of the crime – begins. For those who are found guilty of crimes, societies must find a way to punish them.
5 These punishments range from fines to imprisonment to sometimes even death.

For serious crimes, imprisonment is the most common form of punishment. Prisons serve a variety of purposes. First, governments hope they will act as an external control and discourage other people
10 from committing crimes. This is called the *deterrence* function. The deterrence function also extends to current prisoners. In other words, the experience in prison should discourage them from committing crimes after they leave prison. Imprisonment, as well as other forms of punishment, also satisfies the public's desire for a criminal to be
15 punished. This is called the *retribution* function. Most criminals cannot commit additional crimes while they are in prison; this is the *incapacitation* function. Finally, modern prison programs often try to help criminals change their behaviors so they can reenter society. This is called the *rehabilitation* function.

Does incarceration work?

20 Most experts agree that imprisonment, or *incarceration*, successfully fulfills some of its functions some of the time. For example, most offenders cannot commit crimes against innocent people while they are in prison. Thus, imprisonment protects public safety. When crime rates increase, governments often react by putting more people in
25 prison. In the United States, the prison population grew from under 500,000 in 1980 to about 2.3 million in 2009. The United States has the highest *rate of incarceration* in the world (see Figure 8.1). One major reason for this high rate is that criminals receive longer **sentences** in the United States than in most other countries.

30 However, experts disagree about the success of imprisonment in fulfilling some of its other functions, particularly deterrence and rehabilitation. For some criminals, imprisonment is not a deterrent to crime. Some may actually feel at home in prison. Prison provides a controlled and predictable environment where inmates are clothed,

serve
fulfill
satisfy

sentence time in prison ordered by a court

Figure 8.1. Incarceration rates by country

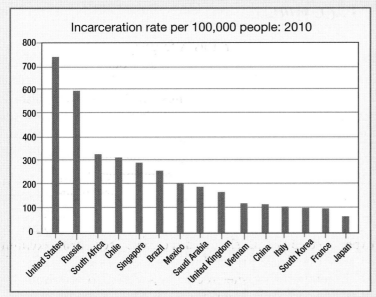

Incarceration rate per 100,000 people: 2010

Source: Kings College, London

35 fed, and told what to do. Outside life may be too difficult for them. Others are accustomed to a life of crime. Crime is their profession, and prison is just part of their job. In addition, most studies suggest that people who go to prison for their crimes are likely to commit another crime. The more crimes they have committed in the past, the
40 more likely they are to commit another crime in the future. A 10-year study by the U.S. Department of Justice of state prisons found that on average, about two-thirds of all former prisoners are arrested for another crime within three years after their release.

The rehabilitation function of prison is perhaps the most
45 controversial. For the public, this function may conflict with its retribution function. Many people do not want the government to use taxpayer money to help offenders. Rehabilitation programs may include drug treatment, job training, counseling, and education. It may also include resocialization, that is, training for how to behave
50 appropriately outside of prison. Some rehabilitation programs can help reduce future crime, but they are not always successful. By their very nature, prisons work against rehabilitation. They force people to be cut off from outside society. The habits and attitudes that prisoners learn may be the exact opposite of those they are supposed to learn.

55 In prison they may learn to accept violence as normal. They will also mix with other criminals and learn new criminal skills. As one author stated, "It is difficult to train for freedom in a cage."

Alternatives to prison

There are some alternatives to prison as a punishment. For example, instead of going to jail, some offenders are put on *probation.* This
60 means that they are allowed to remain in the community under some kind of supervision. They may have to follow certain rules or do some community service, such as cleaning up parks or helping poor people. New technologies, including security bracelets, can assist in this supervision. The security bracelets let the authorities identify the
65 location of offenders at all times. So, for example, offenders may be given probation on the condition that they go nowhere near a certain part of the city, or that they do not leave their house except to go to work. The security bracelets allow the authorities to track the wearers' movements.

The death penalty

70 The ultimate punishment is the death penalty, which is also called *capital punishment.* Many countries have abolished the death penalty. However, according to Amnesty International, in 2009, capital punishment was still in active use in 58 countries. In most countries, it has been used as a punishment for homicide, but some governments
75 have also used it against political enemies.

The death penalty certainly serves the incapacitation function of punishment, and it satisfies the public's desire for retribution. However, is it also a deterrent to potential criminals? Most experts believe it is not. One reason is that the death penalty is often a punishment
80 for crimes of passion, which often occur under the overwhelming pressure of explosive emotion and uncontrollable rage. People who commit these crimes are usually so emotional that they do not stop to think about whether their criminal act might result in the death penalty. In addition, there have been studies in 14 different nations
85 that have produced some surprising findings. The studies show that when the death penalty was abolished in these countries, there was actually a decline in murder rates.

There are many methods of dealing with crime and criminals. However, because each usually has more than one function, some of which are in conflict, the debate on the fairest and most effective ways to reduce crime is likely to continue as long as people continue to commit crimes.

Inside a Prison

One long-serving prisoner described his first impression of prison in the following way: "Entering prison for the first time can be a frightening experience. The noise level is what strikes you, and it is unlike any noise you have ever heard before. It's human noise and clamor. That, coupled with the sight of those dreary bars, made me think, 'Man, what have I gotten myself into here?!' When you enter prison, you have entered a world of its own. . . . Prison is a confined place, packed with living bodies of every shape, color, and size. You will find yourself closer to other human beings than you ever have been before, many of whom you won't like."

1 Making a chart Ⓐ Ⓡ ✄

A Review the text, focusing on functions of the incarceration and capital punishment.

B Make a chart that lists functions of these punishments across the top row. Then decide if they serve these functions.

- Y – Yes
- N – No
- M – Mixed
- DA– Does not apply

The first one has been done for you.

	Incapacitation	deterrence	retribution	Rehabilitation
Incarceration	Y	M	Y	M
Capital Punishment	Y	M	Y	DA

2 Collocations Ⓥ Ⓦ ✄

> You have learned that nouns and verbs often occur together in a collocation. Sometimes there are several nouns and verbs with similar meanings that form similar collocations. However, not every verb can collocate with every noun.

A Scan the text to find the nouns that collocate with the following verbs.

serve _____ – purpose
_____ – function

fulfill _____ funtcion

satisfy _____ desire

B With a partner, study the chart below and answer the questions. The nouns in the second column collocate the most frequently with the verbs in the first column.

Verb	Collocating Nouns
serve	function, need, purpose
fulfill	aim, desire, function, need, objective, purpose
satisfy	desire, need, objective

1. What do the verbs have in common?
2. What do the nouns have in common?

C Write a sentence with each of the three verbs.

3 Applying what you have read Ⓡ Ⓦ

A Discuss in a group: If the people below are found guilty, what, if any, punishment do you think each should receive? Should they be sent to prison? Why or why not? If so, for how long? If not, what should be their punishment?

- A 16-year-old boy is arrested for stealing a car. It is the fourth time he has been arrested for this type of crime.
- A group of young men beat up and robbed an immigrant in his grocery store. They shouted insults about his country while they were hitting him. The shopkeeper recovered, but he was badly hurt.
- An elderly woman was driving under the influence of alcohol. She caused an accident, and someone was killed. It was the first time she had been arrested.
- A 34-year-old man didn't like it when his girlfriend's four-year-old child cried. So he hit the child on the head with a piece of wood. The injury was serious, and she suffered permanent brain damage.
- A man found that $1,000 had been transferred into his bank account by mistake. When the bank discovered the problem, they demanded the return of the money. The man refused. He was charged with stealing $1,000.
- A 22-year-old woman was arrested in a supermarket for shoplifting. The store detective found the following items in her handbag: a lipstick, a child's toy, several cans of food, and three DVDs.
- Two bank robbers shot and killed a police officer when they were trying to get away from the crime scene.
- A 21-year-old woman stole a handbag that had been left in a restaurant. It had $32 in it. She has committed similar crimes in the past. She has a history of drug problems.

B Choose one of the situations and write a short explanation of the punishment and the reasons for your decision.

Chapter 8 Academic Vocabulary Review

The following words appear in the readings in Chapter 8. They all come from the Academic Word List, a list of words that researchers have discovered occur frequently in many different types of academic texts. For a complete list of all the Academic Word List words in this chapter and in all the readings in this book, see the Appendix on pages 213–214.

Reading 1 What Stops Us from Committing Crimes	Reading 2 Science and Technology in Crime Fighting	Reading 3 Crime and Punishment
bonds	analysis	alternatives
colleagues	confirmed	assist
detectives	documents	confine
display	invisible	react
license	sufficient	release (n)
researchers	techniques	ultimate

Complete the sentences with words from the lists.

1. You should store your important _documents_ , such as your passport, in a safe place.
2. When the couple had saved _sufficient_ money, they bought a small apartment.
3. The official _confirmed_ the passenger's identity by checking in the computer.
4. Governments often _assist_ one another in fighting international crime.
5. Scientists use _analysis_ of DNA to identify the people who were at the crime scene.
6. If you get too many traffic tickets, you may lose your driver's _license_ .
7. Government programs train offenders for work after their _release_ from prison.
8. At first, the traces of blood were _invisible_ . They could only be seen with a special light.
9. Scientists are developing new _techniques_ for identification. For example, soon computers will be able to recognize faces in a crowd.
10. The shop _displayed_ its new spring fashions in the front window.
11. The mayor did not like the first building plan, so her staff proposed several _alternatives_ .
12. _Detectives_ are members of the police force who solve crimes.

Practicing Academic Writing

In this text you have learned about various forms of *social control*, that is, ways in which society exerts control over its members and encourages them to conform to its norms. These include socialization of new members as well as many types of sanctions. There are positive sanctions, which reward conformity, and a range of negative sanctions, which punish deviance.

External Controls on Deviant Behavior

Discuss the statement below. Decide if you think it is valid. Support your position with examples.

As a society grows and becomes more complex, it will need a wider range of social controls. Specifically, it will need more formal and stronger external controls in order to continue to function smoothly.

PREPARING TO WRITE

Understanding the Prompt

A Read the introduction and the prompt carefully. Review the guidelines in the Writing Assignment in Chapter 7.

B In order to respond to the prompt you will need to:

- Decide on your point of view, that is, whether you think the statement is valid.
- Explain the terms that you will use.
- Explain what happens when a society becomes more complex. You may want to begin by explaining what a society is like when it is still very small and simple.
- Suggest some forms of stronger, more formal social controls. Two is probably a good number for a short essay. Discuss each in a separate paragraph.
- Give reasons why these stronger controls are (or are not) needed as a society grows. You may want to say what the consequences would be if a large and complex society does *not* develop stronger controls.
- Illustrate your point of view with examples.

C With a classmate, discuss your point of view and how you would explain these points. Make a list of the terms you will explain. Write some notes about your discussion.

D Review the readings to find the terms you will use. Paraphrase these terms. Use the guidelines from Developing Writing Skills at the end of Chapter 5 (page 132) to help you.

E Make a rough outline of your essay. One has been started for you.

I. Introduction

- _____
- _____
- _____

II. Explain what happens when a society grows.

- What is it like when it is small? What forms of social control exist? Give an example.
- What happens as it grows and becomes more complex and diverse? Are the same social controls effective?
- _____

III. Discuss one strong formal social control.

- What is it?
- Why would it be effective (or unnecessary, if you disagree)? Give an example.
- _____

IV. Discuss another strong formal social control.

- What is it?
- Why would it be effective (or unnecessary, if you disagree)? Give an example.

NOW WRITE

A Review the information about introductory paragraphs in "Developing Writing Skills" near the end of Chapter 3 (page 80). Now write your introductory paragraph. Be sure to include all three elements.

- Introduction of your topic
- Your claim about the topic – this should be a restatement of part of the prompt (or the opposite if you disagree)
- Road map for the rest of your essay – what you will say in your body paragraphs

B Review the writing assignment on body paragraphs in Chapter 1 (pages 26 and 27). Now write three body paragraphs based on your outline.

- Remember that every body paragraph should have a topic sentence.
- Be sure to provide examples to illustrate your points.

C Review "After You Write: Conclusions" near the end of Chapter 6 (pages 159–160).

- Be sure your essay ends with a section that concludes smoothly. It can just be two or three sentences.
- Your conclusion should do more than simply restate your main claim.

A Reread your draft and check that:

- It has an introductory paragraph with a general statement and a main idea sentence that states a claim about the topic.
- Each body paragraph has a topic sentence and supporting evidence.
- It has an appropriate conclusion.

Transitions

Writing good paragraphs is important, but it is also important to make sure the paragraphs all fit well together. One way to help all of the pieces fit well is to write a sentence that makes a good transition between one paragraph and another. Good writers try to create a thread that connects the end of one paragraph to the beginning of the next. They may repeat a word or use a synonym to show the connection between the two paragraphs.

Kinds of Connections

- Sometimes each paragraph is an item on a **list**, for example, each paragraph gives a reason or an example. The first sentence in each paragraph may include words such as *first*, *second*, or *most important.*

- Sometimes there is a **contrast** between the two paragraphs. The first sentence in the second paragraph may show this contrast with something in the previous paragraph.

- Sometimes the first paragraph contains a statement, and the next paragraph contains an **explanation** or **expansion** of the statement.

- Sometimes one paragraph presents a **problem** and the next paragraph offers a **solution**.

- Sometimes the relationship between the paragraphs is **cause** and **effect**. The first sentence in the second paragraph may show this relationship.

B Read the text below. Pay special attention to the words in red in the first and last sentences. Describe the connection between the two paragraphs. Write it on the blank line to the left of the paragraph. The first one is done for you.

Forensics is an important part of the criminal justice system. It is the use of science and technology to solve crimes. We think of forensics as a high-tech field with lots of special tools and machines, but actually it has a long history.

expansion The use of science to solve a crime dates back at least 700 years. A Chinese book showed the physical differences between a victim of drowning and a victim of strangulation. Almost 600 years later, in the early 1800s, a Spanish chemist published a book about poisons and how to identify them inside a person's body. In the 1880s, fingerprints began to be used as evidence in crimes. At that time, the techniques and equipment were not very advanced.

_____ Today, some scientists analyze blood, hair, and saliva to find criminals. Others analyze powders and other materials for evidence of drugs or explosives. Some study bones and teeth to estimate the victim's sex, age, and health. All of them use advanced technology.

_____ Technology cannot answer all the questions, however. One problem is that when detectives find dead bodies, sometimes they have been dead a long time. It is hard to tell what has happened to them. Scientists can't tell how long the bodies have been there or how they died.

_____ To solve these problems, forensic scientists have developed a research method that is not as high tech – the "body farm." The farm has about 40 dead bodies lying in the woods and in fields. Scientists observe them to see what happens to them, including the damage from weather, insects, and other wild animals. What they learn from these dead bodies helps them solve future crimes. Forensics is not always as glamorous as it appears to be on television!

C After working with these transitions, reread your draft essay.

- Is there a smooth connection between the paragraphs?
- What is the relationship between the paragraphs?
- Does the final sentence in one paragraph link to the first sentence in the next paragraph?

Make some notes about changes you need to make when you revise.

D Exchange essays with a partner. Review his or her essay.

- Is there an introductory paragraph with a general statement and main idea sentence that gives a general idea of what the rest of the essay will be about? Highlight the road map.
- Does each body paragraph have a topic sentence? Underline them.
- Does the author provide examples to support the claims in the essay?
- Are the transitions between the paragraphs smooth and logical?
- Does the essay have a conclusion that is more than a repetition of the introduction?

E Revise your essay.

- Review your partner's suggestions.
- Review your own notes for revision.
- Make necessary changes.

F Edit your essay.

Read over your essay for spelling mistakes, punctuation errors, subject-verb agreement errors, incorrect use of past tense, and article usage. Make corrections if you find errors.

Appendix

Academic Word List vocabulary

abandon
abnormal
academic
access
accessible
accuracy
achieve
achievement
adequate
adult
adulthood
affect
aid
alternative
analysis
approach
appropriate
approximate
area
aspect
assist
assume
attachment
attitude
attribute
author
authority
available
aware
bias
bond
capable
category
challenge
chapter
chemical
circumstance
civil
colleague
comment
commit
commitment
communicate
communication

community
compensation
complex
complexity
computer
concentration
concept
conclude
confine
confirm
conflict
conform
conformity
consequence
consequently
considerable
consist
consistent
constant
consumer
contrast
contribute
contribution
controversial
cooperation
corporate
couple
create
creation
creativity
credit
cultural
culture
currency
cycle
data
debate
decade
decline
define
definition
depression
detect
detection

detective
device
devote
discrimination
display
distinct
document
dominant
dominate
drama
economic
economy
eliminate
emerge
emergent
emphasize
enforcement
enforce
enhance
enormous
environment
equate
equation
equipment
estimate
ethical
ethnicity
evidence
exclude
expand
expert
external
factor
feature
finally
financial
flexibility
focus
foundation
founder
function
fundamental
furthermore
gender

generation
globally
goal
grade
highlighted
identical
identification
identify
identity
ignore
illegal
illustrate
image
immigrant
impact
impose
imposition
inaccessible
incline
income
indicate
individual
individualism
initial
injured
injury
institution
institutional
integrated
intelligence
intense
interact
interactive
internal
interpret
investigate
investing
invisible
involve
involvement
irrational
isolate
issue
item

job	percent	rely	summary
labor	percentage	require	survey
lecture	period	research	survive
legal	persist	researcher	symbol
license	persistent	resource	task
link	perspective	respond	team
location	physical	respondent	techniques
maintain	physically	response	technological
major	policy	reveal	technology
majority	positive	revolution	temporarily
mature	potential	revolutionary	tense
media	precede	role	text
medium	predict	secure	theory
mental	predictable	security	topic
method	previous	seek	trace
military	primarily	sex	traditional
minimize	process	sexism	transfer
minor	professional	shift	transform
minority	prohibit	significant	transmit
negative	promote	similar	trend
networking	psychological	similarly	ultimate
neutral	psychologist	site	underlying
norm	publication	sole	unique
normal	publish	somewhat	unpredictable
normally	purchase	source	variation
nuclear	pursue	specific	vary
obvious	range	statistics	version
occupation	ratio	status	violate
occur	react	strategy	violation
overall	regulation	stress	visible
paragraph	reinforce	stressful	whereas
participate	release	structure	widespread
participation	relevant	style	
passive	reliable	subordinate	
perceive	reliant	sufficient	

Skills index

Credits

Text Credits

Pages 29–30, 42–44, 57–58. Thio, A. *Sociology: A brief introduction,* Seventh Edition. Boston: Pearson Education Inc., pp. 44–45, 228–229, 408–409.

Page 84. Housework graph adapted from *Exactly How Much Housework Does a Husband Create?,* University of Michigan Insitute of Social Research, April 3, 2008. Used by permission of Institute for Social Research, University of Michigan.

Page 93. Life expectancy graph adapted from *United Nations, World Population Prospects: The 2008 Revision* (2009). Used by permission of United Nations.

Illustration Credits

Page 74: Eric Olson

Page 83: "Bizarro" used with the Dan Piraro, King Features Syndicate and the Cartoonist Group. All rights reserved.

Page 98, 193: Carly Monardo

Page 99: Clay Bennett / © 2002 The Christian Science Monitor (www.CSMonitor.com). Reprinted with permission.

Page 171: ©www.mchumor.com

Photography Credits

1 ©BananaStock/Thinkstock; 3 *(left to right)* ©TonyV3112/ Shutterstock; ©Digital Vision/Thinkstock; ©Radius/ SuperStock; 5 ©FotoFlirt/Alamy; 8 ©Caroline Penn/Age Fotostock; 15 ©Ariel Skelley/Blend Images; 21 *(top to bottom)* ©David Sacks/Lifesize/Thinkstock; ©AP Photo/Evan Agostini; ©Hill Street Studios/Blend Images; 29 ©Marka/ SuperStock; 30 ©Buccina Studios/Photodisc/Thinkstock; 32 ©Kim Steele/Blend Images/Alamy; 35 ©Gabriela Medina/ Blend Images/Getty Images; 36 ©iStockphoto/Thinkstock; 39 ©Masterfile; 40 *(top to bottom)* ©Robert Harding Picture Library/SuperStock; ©Alexander Joe/AFP/Getty Images; 41 ©Emmanuel Dunand/AFP/Getty Images; 43 ©AP Photo/Dean Hoffmeyer/Richmond; 44 ©John Rowley/ Stone/Getty Images; 53 ©Blend Images/SuperStock; 56 *(left to right)* ©Daniel Padavona/Shutterstock; ©Jirasaki/ Shutterstock; ©Simple stock shots/Punchstock; 57 *(left to right)* ©iStockphoto/Thinkstock; ©Design Pics/PunchStock; 63 ©KidStock/Blend Images/Getty Images; 66 ©Jon Feingersh/Blend Images/Getty Images; 71 ©Wavebreak Media/Thinkstock; 75 ©Kyu Oh/iStockphoto; 82 ©Kurhan/ Shutterstock; 85 ©Chip Somodevilla/Getty Images; 102 ©iStockphoto/Thinkstock; 109 ©A. Chederros/ONOKY - Photononstop/Alamy; 113©Andy Dean Photography/ Shutterstock; 114 ©Ian Dagnall/Alamy; 118 ©Mark Bowden/ iStockphoto; 120 ©Nicholas Kamm/AFP/Getty Images; 121 ©Mark Makela/ZUMA Press/Corbis; 124 ©Wiskerke/ Alamy; 125 ©AP Photo/Lewis Whyld; 126 ©Paul Bradbury/ OJO Images/Getty Images; 127 ©Mirrorpix/Courtesy Everett Collection; 129 ©Robert Daly/Age Fotostock; 141 ©Brad Walker/SuperStock/Alamy; 144 ©EPA/Felipe Trueba; 150 ©Brand X Pictures/Thinkstock; 161 ©Burke/Triolo Productions/Brand X Pictures/Thinkstock; 166 ©Yvonne Hemsey/Getty Images; 167 ©AP Photo/Virginia State Police; 173 ©Allesalltag Bildagentur/Age Fotostock; 176 ©AP Photo/Alexandre Meneghini; 179 ©Michael Willis/Alamy; 180 ©Andrew Paterson/Alamy; 189 ©Bersanelli/Shutterstock; 193 *(left to right)* ©Cliff Lipson/CBS/Getty Images; ©Bob Daemmrich/Alamy; 194 ©Jeffrey Coolidge/The Image Bank/Getty Images; 195 *(top to bottom)* ©Andy Crawford/ Dorling Kindersley/Gettty Images; ©Dr. P.Marazzi/Science Photo Library/Getty Images; 196 ©Bettmann/Corbis; 200 ©Hemera/Thinkstock; 205 ©Slobo/iStockphoto